T0327254

2013

Editors
Sidney Gottlieb and Richard Allen

Editorial Advisory Board
Charles Barr   Thomas L. Leitch
James Naremore   David Sterritt
Michael Walker

Founding Editor
Christopher Brookhouse

Editorial Associate
Renata Jackson

Cover Design
Deborah Dutko

We evaluate manuscripts for the *Hitchcock Annual* throughout the year. Send correspondence and submissions to either Sidney Gottlieb, Department of Communications and Media Studies, Sacred Heart University, Fairfield, CT 06825 or Richard Allen, Department of Cinema Studies, New York University, Tisch School of the Arts, 721 Broadway, 6th floor, New York, NY 10003. E-mail addresses: spgottlieb@aol.com or Richard.Allen@nyu.edu

We invite articles on all aspects of Hitchcock's life, works, and influence, and encourage a variety of critical approaches, methods, and viewpoints. For all submissions, follow the guidelines of the *Chicago Manual of Style*, using full notes rather than works cited format. If submitting by mail, send two copies (only one of which will be returned) and return postage. But we prefer submissions via e-mail, which makes it easier to circulate essays for editorial review. The responsibility for securing any permissions required for publishing material in the essay rests with the author. Illustrations may be included, but as separate TIFF files rather than as part of the text file. Decision time is normally within three months. The submission of an essay indicates your commitment to publish it, if accepted, in the *Hitchcock Annual*, and that it is not simultaneously under consideration for publication elsewhere.

For all orders, including back issues, contact Columbia University Press, 61 West 62nd Street, New York, NY 10023; www.columbia/edu/cu/cup

The *Hitchcock Annual* is indexed in the *Film Literature Index* and *MLA International Bibliography*.

Columbia University Press   *New York*

Columbia University Press
Publishers Since 1893
New York   Chichester, West Sussex

Copyright © 2013 Sidney Gottlieb/*Hitchcock Annual*
All rights reserved

ISBN 978-0-231-16367-5 (pbk. : alk. paper)
ISSN 1062-5518

∞

Columbia University Press books are printed on
permanent and durable acid-free paper.
This book is printed on paper with recycled content.

Printed in the United States of America

p 10 9 8 7 6 5 4 3 2 1

References to Internet Web sites (URLs) were accurate at the
time of writing. Neither the editors nor Columbia University
Press are responsible for URLs that may have expired or
changed since the manuscript was prepared

HITCHCOCK ANNUAL
2013

AMY SARGEANT

Champagne *(1928): The Nation's Favorite Meets the Critics' Choice*

The British Film Institute's recent restoration and screening of *Champagne*, with a newly-commissioned score from Mira Calix, provides an opportune moment for the reappraisal of a somewhat neglected film.[1] Such attention it has received has tended to discourage further critical engagement. I am as interested in examining the reasons for this neglect as in offering an endorsement of the film's various merits. The Hitchcock scholars Charles Barr and John Russell Taylor have judged *Champagne* unfavorably against the earlier 1928 release, *The Farmer's Wife*.[2] Hitchcock himself seemingly acquiesced to Truffaut's suggestion that *Champagne* was lacking in plot,[3] and reputedly disparaged the talents of its star: according to Michael Powell, Hitchcock considered Betty Balfour "a piece of suburban obscenity . . . England's ersatz Mary Pickford."[4] Raymond Durgnat, while appreciating *Champagne*'s finer moments, succinctly determined that:

> Hitchcock does what he can to cover up for a story for that's neither fish, flesh, fowl, nor good red herring, using bold details and emphatic confrontations to distract us from a plot which is not only improbable but creates a very tricky oscillation as between suspense and comedy. The idea is presumably that a certain fascinating be-puzzlement as to the oscillations between a certain suspense and a certain san fairy ann will rivet us to the superficialities and put the underlying logic in its proper place, out of mind.[5]

This is a fair enough comment, as far as it goes—but more, I reckon, does get done in the film than Durgnat and other commentators have been prepared to acknowledge. On the one hand, *Champagne* is a star vehicle, comparable to the casting of Ivor Novello in *The Lodger* (1926) and *Downhill* (1927), its oscillations in tone between not just suspense and comedy but between different registers of comedy catering to (even predicated by) Balfour's range of talents. On the other hand, *Champagne* finds Hitchcock experimenting with various narrative and stylistic devices to which he returns in subsequent films. In terms of Hitchcock's silent films, *Champagne* endorses his preoccupations with "chase" endings and triangulated love stories. It merits appraisal within the canon rather than being cast aside as somehow aberrant or subordinate.

Here, I intend to follow Tom Ryall's example, discussing the film in the context of debates in Britain in the 1920s around "film culture" and "national identity," while disagreeing with his provisional conclusion that a "radical separation" of "art" and "commercial" cinema hindered the creation of "a more aesthetically interesting entertainment cinema in Britain during the interwar years."[6] In other words, I find evidence, not least, but not only, in Hitchcock for such an interaction, while simultaneously finding more interest, not least aesthetic, in British cinema of the 1920s. I draw attention to what Hitchcock's films shared with a usual and general 1920s output rather than itemizing what may be thought to be distinctively unique to Hitchcock. Provisionally, I should like to emphasize a Hitchcockian inheritance, stylistic and thematic, from films on which Hitchcock served an apprenticeship, as assistant director and otherwise, with Graham Cutts, and from other Cutts films. I shall be referring especially to two other Betty Balfour vehicles, Cutts's *The Sea Urchin* (1926; made for Gainsborough) and Geza von Bolvary's even more neglected *Bright Eyes* (1929; known in France as *Palace de Luxe* [fig. 1]) and in

Figure 1

Germany as *Champagner,* a co-production between British International Pictures and the Austrian company Sascha), by way of the film's story and setting, its production context, and a shifting climate of reception in Britain, reinforcing the European dimension of *Champagne.* Furthermore, with the "golden curls" of Daisy (the daughter of the house), the eponymous lodger's sister (seen dancing, in flashback), and the pictures supplied by the lodger's landlady in *The Lodger,* and with Alice (Anny Ondra) in *Blackmail* (1929), *Champagne* confirms an early Hitchcockian fascination with benighted blondes. However, while in *Champagne* Hitchcock makes something of a joke at the blonde's expense (using her to his story's advantage), he accords her a considerable degree of agency: she displays initiative and resilience; she is not merely a victim.[7]

Story and Setting

While Hitchcock's *Downhill* (made for Gainsborough) is the story of a poor little rich boy (and a father's tough treatment of his innocent son), *Champagne* (made for British International Pictures) is the story of a poor little rich girl (and a father's tough treatment of his somewhat spoilt yet willful and sometimes mischievous daughter). A routine, generic, plot is seemingly announced, in the manner of Murnau's *Sunrise* (1927), in the non-naming of characters in *Champagne*'s opening credits: The Girl, The Boy, The Man, The Father. The scenario, however, is somewhat more baffling (and, at times, even discomforting), serving alongside the film's spectacular attractions and distractions to defer delivery of a predictable romantic dénouement. It seems worth describing the scenario at some length, offering something of a reading (Durgnat's cursory rendition skimped and evidently found less delight in detail than did Truffaut).

The daughter, Betty ("The Girl": Betty Balfour), of an American millionaire (Gordon Harker), hires a pilot to fly her to the ship on which she intends to join her boyfriend, John ("The Boy": Jean Bradin). To much excitement, a lifeboat is launched to save her from the sea. Meanwhile, "The Man," credited as Theo van Alten, is eye-balled by an apparent floozie soliciting his gaze in preference to the older gentleman companion stroking her arm—in whom she shows little interest (drowsy old men and any number of eye-balling younger women on the make also appearing in *Bright Eyes*): it may be that she regards him as a prospective better catch; it may be that her wry and lopsided smile connotes a recognition of him as her equal (a lounge lizard) or her adversary as a detective hired to keep watch over personnel on board.[8] A cut suggests that he catches her eye, but this mysterious man turns aside (refusing her intensive, steady stare), distracted by the commotion surrounding the launch of the lifeboat. Once aboard, the Girl, catching sight of the Boy, cautions him not to recognize her (their exchanged look already noted by the Man) but later he comes to her cabin (again, observed by the Man). She kisses and embraces the Boy, jumps for joy, and kicks her heels in the air in delight at her ability to engineer an elopement: "Wouldn't I love to see dear Daddy's face" — and she has scuppered his airplane. As in *Young and Innocent* (1937), a daughter adventurously seizes fate in her own hands, effecting an escape in defiance of the authority carried by her father: both girls have "nerve." In *Champagne*, however, news of the story has already reached Betty's father, who sits nervously twitching and chewing a cigar at his desk, reading his paper. He peremptorily dispatches further attention from a black servant delivering messages and a barrage of demanding newspaper reporters and photographers (matching the pack of newshounds surrounding Larita at the beginning and end of *Easy Virtue* [1927] and the equally unwelcome intrusions of society gossip columnists at the opening of *Notorious* [1946]: "Mata Hari — she's good for the papers," Alicia duly, dryly, comments).

That night, there is business on deck involving a makeshift, ill-fitting engagement ring, a feather fan, and a wind machine (again, observed by the Man — who gallantly cloaks the Girl in the Boy's spare overcoat). With "Cupid at the prow, but Neptune at the helm," the rolling of the boat (the camera rocking — a device to be repeated less exaggeratedly in *Rich and Strange* [1932]) obliges the Girl to lurch down to luncheon: Balfour and Bradin convincingly stumble, as if thrown off balance. She (looking queasy) is joined at her table by the Man (previously sitting alone, strong-stomached and in waiting, the first to arrive in the restaurant). The Boy duly descends, even more queasily, passing a stuffed, glazed, and decorated pig's head amidst a crowded buffet spread, and turns back. A bell-boy, with better sea legs, scuttles past him downstairs and delivers Marconi telegrams to the Man and the Girl. The Girl reads a warning from her Father that the Boy (any boy — ?) can only be after her inheritance: "DOES LIFE MEAN NOTHING TO YOU THAT YOU RISK IT FOR THAT CAKE HOUND YOUR BOULEVARD SHEIK IS ONLY AFTER MY BANK ROLL." The Man greets this news with a characteristic sinisterly arched eyebrow, directed at the Girl. There is more business with stormily swaying doors as the Girl returns to the Boy and reveals the contents of the telegram. The Boy feels insulted by the Father and affronted by the Girl, who pertinently and legitimately argues that her money afforded her the luxury to fly halfway round the globe to meet him. She informs him that she has arranged for the ship's captain to marry them. She thinks that "money entitles her to do anything," complains the Boy, and has presumed a prerogative on both counts: "Don't I have a say?"

The ensuing romantic tiff—and the removal of the ring from the Girl's thumb—is comedically frustrated by further lurching and rocking: the ring gets dropped and the Boy fumbles around to retrieve it (the Girl and the Boy are physically pitched together, outside of their control, despite their temperamental distance, in contrast to *The 39 Steps* [1935], where a putative romantic couple finds itself circumstantially shackled). However, as per plan, the protagonists of *Champagne* all arrive safely in Paris, by way of the Cherbourg Express (conveyed by stock shots of the Eiffel Tower, the Place de la Concorde, and the Arc de Triomphe). The Girl immediately embarks on "revelry," buying "snappy gowns," devising "knock-out" cocktails and, more significantly, flamboyantly showing off her purchases and concoctions to the entertainment of an ensemble of friends, including her erstwhile shipmate, the Man. One cocktail is extravagantly wasted, tipped to camera into the fireplace. The Boy arrives, with flowers, apologizing for a week's absence, only to say, again, that simplicity would be in better taste: he is already something of an ally, unwittingly or otherwise, in the Father's agenda. The Girl pretends contrition (making amends at someone else's expense and laughing in the Boy's face); the Man flatters the Girl (asked which of the "attractive creations" modeled he prefers, he disconcertingly, somewhat flirtatiously, says that the wearer, undoubtedly, is "the most charming"). A puckered mouth, in close-up, announces the arrival of her father at the door (Cutts's *The White Shadow* [1924] features a strong physical attachment of a father to his daughter, while in *The Sea Urchin*, "the girl" leaps into and is

carried in her "fathers'" laps). Betty is told that all is lost—
"we're ruined"—and the modest dress she has portentously
borrowed is, indeed, in keeping with their new station in life.
Betty imagines the mockery of her fine-weather "friends" at
her downfall. The Boy wants to comfort her but she rejects
him in favor of her Father, who says that the Boy's departure
was to be expected; the Man, a potential rival for the Girl's
affections, kisses the Girl's hand (he astutely provides suave,
emollient reassurance and verbal conciliation when the Boy is
verbally harsh and gauchely uncertain in his attempts to offer
physical comfort).

The Girl volunteers to sell all her jewels, but the jewels are
stolen from her by an anonymous street thief. Father and
daughter frugally set up home together in a Paris garret,
where the Girl struggles at housekeeping and proves herself a
willing but lousy cook (affording opportunities for slapstick).
The Father finds her burnt offerings inedible, pleads a loss of
appetite but instead (one plate on the garret table fading and
cutting to another with the camera pulling back to reveal a
different background) eats a lavish lunch at a restaurant: after
all, this is only an elaborate (and costly) hoax, intended to
teach his daughter a lesson, in which the audience is made
complicit long before the surprise is revealed to Betty. The Boy
returns and offers to "take her away from all this," but she
continues to swear loyalty to her father (they have their pride,
she insists, at his suggestion that he could look after them
both). His petulant rejoinder to her insistence that she will
earn her own living is that she will make a mess of it—"as
everything you lay your hands on." Resourcefully, the Girl
seeks employment—anything—and unashamedly, she takes a
job at a cabaret: "I used to pay to come to places like this—
now they pay me"—where, she is yet warned (and fears)
"anything might happen." Again, she encounters the Man,
and then the Boy, who fears that she was sitting at the Man's
table and demands another for himself. "It's bad enough to
find you here—worse that you are enjoying it," the Boy
protests. Again, she proudly raises her chin at the Boy,
asserting her independence: after a moment's pause, she

capriciously commences to shimmy in her seat, mockingly resisting his admonishing address (she is more interested in the music than in hearing what he says, perhaps, or maybe in a bold attempt at hilarity), while the Man continues to observe the couple from a distance. Having melodramatically escaped the imagined lustful advances of the Man, she proceeds jokily to defy the presumption of control advanced by the Boy.

The Boy then returns with reinforcement: Betty's father, who accuses her of disgracing him. Thoroughly confused, betrayed, and humiliated, she desperately accepts the Man's offer of help, arriving at his luxurious apartment at an irregular hour and asking him to take her home to America (thus aligning the Man with her Father). Together, they take a train to the harbor (the Girl still looking somewhat perturbed and apprehensive), while the Boy drives furiously in pursuit, hoping to catch them (echoing the closing chase sequence of *The Lodger* and anticipating the closing chase of *Blackmail*). *Champagne* thus at least squares a familiar triangle (complicatedly foreshadowed in *The Sea Urchin* by an orphanage doctor and a potential father-in-law both acting as surrogate father figures, in addition to a con-man, between times, expediently posing as "father" to "the girl" as a means of exploitation). In *Champagne*, both the Boy and Girl have been tested by the Father's intermediary—the Man ("PREVENT MARRIAGE . . . ELOPE WITH HER YOURSELF IF NECESSARY. CAN TRUST HER TO YOU," reads the Man's telegram from his friend, the Father, it is finally revealed)—while the Boy sides with the Father even as he peevishly bids to retain the Girl's love. In anticipation of the film's dénouement, the Boy confirms himself a worthy son-in-law by his endorsement of the Father's position, being both protective and controlling. The Girl is the last to know that she has been fooled and made a figure of fun (the Father, the Man, and the Boy have conspired to take advantage of her). At the end, the comedy is of the manner of bedroom farce (she inadvertently hits the Boy over the head with a towel rail before kissing him in surprise and relief), with the retention of a vestigial sense of menace. *Champagne*'s closing pursuit echoes its opening escape. The

Father seals a reconciliation between Man and Boy with a firm handshake and blesses the reunion of Boy and Girl—who joshingly bicker over who will arrange for the captain to marry them on their way to New York. It is never explicitly stated that the Father's friend (the Man in whose trust he places his daughter) is a private detective; at times his spying seems no less ominously voyeuristic than that of the Neuilly orphanage caretaker (by way of keyholes rather than portholes) of his young charges in *The Sea Urchin*. In *Champagne*, the Girl expresses appropriate (but remarkable) compliance, in finding the funny side of her father's mischief-making and management of her affairs: after all, he *will* (she teases), despite everything, provide another airplane, as the Father (in a parody of despair) shakes his head in his hands. The couple is toasted—with champagne.

In August 1928, the trade paper *The Bioscope* set the agenda for subsequent lukewarm critical appraisals: "Though the interest at times is thin, it never flags. It is a picture which may not rouse great enthusiasm, but may be depended upon to please every class of audience."[9] One of the means by which Hitchcock prevents the interest from flagging is his incorporation in *Champagne* of pictorial material in the diegesis as a substitute for written exposition, in emulation of concurrent German practice (as in Murnau's *The Last Laugh* [1924]). In *Blackmail*, Alice feverishly imagines a neon advertising sign above Piccadilly Circus morphing into a stabbing knife. In *The Ring* (1927), an unraveling roll of tickets shows time passing and the great number of punters flocking to Jack's fight; the size of lettering and his place on the bill chart Jack's rise to the top of his profession. *The Lodger* actively opens with the dissemination of news (the writing, printing, and selling of papers on newsstands) and the gossip it promotes, "Murder—Wet from the Press," while in *Easy Virtue* the discovery of Larita's "vile secret" by her new mother-in-law is prompted by recognition of Larita from photographs in a newspaper of Larita at a polo match. Maps of London are subsequently deployed as an instrument of investigation, tracking the Avenger's nocturnal activities; as in

Rich and Strange and *Young and Innocent, Champagne* features newspaper headlines ("Flying Heiress Rouses Father's Wrath"), telegrams, menu cards, shop and station signage, and handwritten notes. The theatrical agent's secretary takes down shorthand which dissolves into Betty's letter of introduction being punched out on a typewriter (one amongst many of the hopeful applicants whose pictures adorn the agency's walls).

In 1921, Hitchcock contributed an article to the trade journal *The Motion Picture Studio*, commenting that

> the first and most important aim is to make a title readable. . . . Bad titles can harm a picture, they create an indifferent atmosphere, and look shoddy. Good titles will create a harmonious setting, and help the picture to run smoothly."[10]

Champagne answered Hitchcock's call for well-balanced, hand-lettered, economical dialogue titles, with embellishments (unlike *The Lodger*) confined to decorated capitals, uniformly white on a flat black ground. As in *Bright Eyes, Champagne*'s titles are pithy and sometimes witty in themselves, adding to the film's entertainment value, sometimes predictive. For instance, Betty's speculation of "Daddy's face" (in a confiding dialogue title) summons that face—for the film's audience. Mostly, the titles convey dialogue, with minimal, occasional scene-setting: "Paris—revelry." In the later 1920s, Hitchcock proved himself especially ingenious (too ingenious, said more churlish critics) in his pursuit of a general trend, in Britain as elsewhere, to reduce the number of interpolated title cards.[11]

Temporal and spatial shifts in continuity are rendered economically and with ease, with modernist efficiency. There is a nifty dissolve, simultaneously conveying Betty's newfound interest in household management, from her shaking out of a plain bedsheet to her laying of a checkered tablecloth. The camera closes in to reveal the contents of Betty's jewelry case; there is then a cut to a shallow set with a smooth track camera right, parallel to the picture plane, shot from the waist down, showing her carrying the case on the street. She passes a man in shabby trousers, loitering in a doorway. The man pursues her and snatches the case. The camera briefly pauses on Betty, then tracks back in the opposite direction, ending on the case on the pavement, open and empty. *Rich and Strange* duly presented figures on deck by way of a shot leveled at their lower legs stepping across rope; *Strangers on a Train* (1951) was to introduce its protagonists with a low traveling shot directed at legs rushing across a railway platform. In *Champagne*, Betty's wistful recollection of her time aboard ship (the outward presentation of a scene located in her imagination), summoned by a newspaper ad for Cunard, freezes and prompts the camera to pull back to reveal the same shot, mounted, framed, and labeled Aquitania, in a shop window display, around the corner from the agency at which Betty, grimacing, volunteers her beautiful teeth as an advertisement for "Minto."[12] As with heart-shaped biscuits in *The Lodger* (and as does von Bolvary, with cake, in *Bright Eyes*), in *Champagne* Hitchcock "says it with flour" (the girl leaving smudgy handprints on the boy's back when he comes to visit her in her garret—for once, his mocking of her rebounds on him).

Hitchcock's original plot for *Champagne* was less typically a Balfour vehicle than the Walter Mycroft outline eventually adopted. According to John Russell Taylor, the studio wanted something lighter:

> [Hitchcock] elaborated a plot which would turn on the experiences of a girl making a humble living nailing down the lids of champagne crates in Reims, who goes to Paris, gets to live for a while the high life with the champagne she has never actually tasted before, is "ruined" and becomes a sort of high-class whore, and finally, disillusioned with night-clubs, parties and men returns to her old job in Reims, hating the stuff. The story was a bit moralistic.[13]

Given the frequency with which Balfour was likened to Pickford, Mycroft/Stannard/Hitchcock may also have had in mind Maurice Tourneur's *Poor Little Rich Girl* (1917), a typical Pickford vehicle in its combination of comedy and pathos, in which the heroine is more deserving of sympathy than rebuke.

Many British films and British collaborations of the 1920s deploy opposing, socially distinct milieux in their settings as much as their plots. Denison Clift's *Paradise* (1928) follows a vicar's daughter (Balfour) from the home counties to the French Riviera (where she apprehends a jewel thief) courtesy of a prize-winning entry to a crossword competition. In *The Passionate Adventure* (Graham Cutts, 1924), *The Lodger*, *Alley Cat* (Hanns Steinhoff, 1929), and *Piccadilly* (E.A. Dupont, 1929), the opposition is mapped onto London's axis, historically associating a dark East End with production and the bright lights of the West End with consumption.[14] Journeys across London feature in *Blackmail* (through Piccadilly Circus) and in *Sabotage* (1936) (culminating in Piccadilly Circus). Furthermore, *Champagne* (in its differentiation of decks aboard ship, as in *Rich and Strange*), *Bright Eyes,* and *Piccadilly* deploy a vertical axis within a particular setting to articulate class status. Valentine Wilmot's club in *Piccadilly* is clearly descendingly stratified, with restaurant set against kitchen and kitchen set against scullery (duly underlining the ascent of a mere scullery maid to the dance floor); *Bright Eyes* is socially articulated by the cabaret (front of house) being set against the operations of the kitchen and sill room (from which Jenny sets out on her adventure, stacking champagne bottles into ice buckets from a perpetual conveyor belt).

In both *Piccadilly* and *Bright Eyes*, below-stairs staff are discouraged from interrupting their work or amusing themselves (at the management's supposed expense) with self-supplied entertainments (dancing, playing the harmonica with extemporized percussive accompaniment); rather, they need to work faster, "put some of that jazz" into their work. Jenny, latterly as the cabaret companion of the Argentinian millionaire, Gomez (Marcel Vibert), retaliates by ordering the bullying *maître d'*, Monsieur Henri (a match for the despised *maître d'* in *Champagne*), who has fired her for theft, to work quicker, too. In *Bright Eyes*, Jenny (Balfour), typically, lives in an attic far above the club and the lights of a Metro station and its adjacent bars—immediately below the roof—and we see the club's flashing "CHAMPAGNE" lights through the small window in her dingy, meagerly furnished room (comparable to *Champagne*'s "wretched" garret)—in which, in fantasy, she entertains Jean (Jack Trevor), waiter 27. Indeed, *Bright Eyes* opens with a stylized sign, evoking the much-celebrated, Europeanized, American dancer Josephine Baker, rotating to foreground the bare utilitarian structure, the apparatus, which supports it.[15]

In *Champagne*, the kitchen staff in the Paris cabaret handle food roughly: bread rolls are dropped on the floor and then taken to restaurant tables where they are elegantly served by waiters handling tongs to the restaurant's more privileged clientele. The glamour is superficial, merely a show—much of Hitchcock's original moralistic stance survives. While it is mostly directed at Betty, there is also pointed commentary on class and the sham luxury that wealth can purchase. In both *Champagne* (in Betty's social descent) and *Bright Eyes* (in Jenny's social ascent), Balfour's character affiliates herself with staff bullied by an overweening *maître d'*. In *Bright Eyes*, the millionaire cares little for the dance hall's snobby rejection of a girl risen from the sill room; in *Champagne*, Betty disingenuously, or mischievously, gives flowers to the men of the orchestra rather than to the paying clientele and stamps on the *maître d'*'s foot when he pinches her arm and urges her back to work. Betty in *Champagne* is the female equivalent of the gigolo in *Downhill*, marking the necessary acceptance of jobs below the status to which both figures have hitherto been accustomed, before their rehabilitation. Social snobbery returned as a Hitchcockian theme in *Easy Virtue*, with various members of an aristocratic family rejecting the divorcée whom a son marries without their consent, and in *The Skin Game*, where a woman's past is revealed in order to coerce a rival family into submission.

There is more than a suggestion in *Champagne* (as in *The Sea Urchin*) that the girls at the cabaret are required and expected to provide services beyond acting as dancing partners and presenting "men in evening dress" with kissed buttonholes: "For a beginner you sure know how to pick 'em kid," advises a dancer in the company of an older man. Betty's hysterical imagining of what might constitute the "anything" that "could happen to a girl like you in a place like this," shot under the cast shadow of a low-slung, fringed lightshade, is conjured by her earlier sighting of a couple locked in an embrace in one of the private booths lining the dance floor. It is more immediately cued by the serving of a cocktail, called, she is informed, "a maiden's prayer." Betty's bright eyes dart to and fro, following the shaking of the drink. Again, the Man's piercing gaze is accompanied with an arched eyebrow, as he lays his hand over hers. A close-up of Betty's anxious face cuts to a similar booth, in which Betty is seized and assaulted by the Man, whom she pushes away before rushing back to their table on the dance floor, the sequined chiffon shawl (which she wears in the "interiorizing" shots framing the fantasy) torn from her shoulders. Is the Man or is he not "a maiden's prayer" — is he a guardian of her virginity or a threat to her maidenhood?

One of the means whereby the film was deemed likely to "please every class of audience" was *Champagne*'s recycling of a familiar rags and riches fable, especially as carried by Betty Balfour. Notably, these social transformations could be effected in either direction. In the four Squibs films, directed by George Pearson, Balfour played a Piccadilly flower girl, Amelia "Squibs" Hopkins, accompanied by her policeman boyfriend, Charlie (in itself a model for the scenarios of Hitchcock's *The Lodger*, *Blackmail*, and *Sabotage*) and her lovable-rogue-of-a–father, the bookie, Sam. By luck and wit she ascends the social scale, while always, endearingly, keeping her feet on the ground. The last, *Squibs' Honeymoon* (1923), related the story so far:

Squibs, whose escapades as Flower Girl, Calcutta Sweep winner, milk vendor and MP had astonished even herself, felt that after all the simple life was best . . . So she resigned her seat in Parliament, fixed the wedding day with ex-policeman sweetheart Charlie Lee and joined her milk business with that of her old opponent, but now staunch friend, Miss Fitzbulge.[16]

Before being informed of her win in *Squibs Wins the Calcutta Sweep* (1922), Balfour appears in "cod finery" with a basket adorned with a feather on her head. "If you want to marry me, she informs Charlie, "you'd better be quick . . . I might choose a PRINCE." In *Bright Eyes*, Jenny sets her cap at an undeserving waiter—initially drawn by the flirtatious attentions of the svelte, silk-stockinged dancer Lola (Vivian Gibson), the kept woman of a drowsy baron, whose mannered flourishing of a boa, ostentatious smiling, and fluttering of eyelashes Jenny mimics behind her back, using a plain scarf, to the amusement of her fellow kitchen colleagues. Balfour acts out a rise in social class as a comedy "turn" in anticipation of its narrative achievement. The disgraced Jenny comes to the attention of a South American millionaire by chance—she is hiding under his table and she shrieks when he stamps on her hand. He assumes that she has been hired as a surprise attraction and, emboldened by champagne, Jenny does not disappoint his expectations (she can both sing and dance): with the aid of one of Lola's dresses, she is toasted as the best little artiste in Paris (in a vast mirror, Jenny wonders at her own transformation). As in *Champagne*, Balfour's social transformation is accompanied by a change of costume. But Jenny rejects the millionaire's testing proposal of marriage: they both know it is Jean whom she loves and a suitably humbled Jean ultimately recognizes Jenny's worth, which exceeds the superficial trappings of silk, spangles, and feathers (as in Betty's displays of finery in *Champagne*). He has meanwhile been put in his own place by the snobby Lola (his presence in the apartment subsidized by the Baron is duplicitously explained as waitering). The kitchen staff

Figure 2

(especially one fond *sous-chef*—Buttons to her Cinderella—in whom Jenny confides as a friend but who holds a particular torch for her) applaud and invest in Jenny's advancement: it speaks for them all in achieving recognition, while other staff are complicit in or suffer in Jenny's betrayal (she is reported to the police for stealing a single bottle of champagne, intended for the private supper, from the kitchen—while bottles are expendably juggled as mere toy things in the restaurant, dodging a suitably stony-faced Buster Keaton figure). *Bright Eyes* poignantly contrasts sweetness with bitterness. Given the offer of a millionaire, Jenny (like Squibs) remains affiliated by class and loyal to her heart.

In *Champagne*, the "rags to riches" presentiment is reversed, with Betty giving one of her own dresses to the delivery girl from the boutique from which she has made her numerous purchases, only to borrow the same girl's dowdy outfit once she is admonished by her fiancé for her extravagance. As Betty appears in the connecting doorway of her hotel suite as Little Orphan Annie, with a shawl over her head and mock shivering as she raises her eyes skywards and throws torn-paper snowflakes into the air, the poor girl, in her petticoat, is seen in the background (fig. 2): Balfour, as Betty, ironically parodies pathos. Christine Gledhill accordingly observes that "it is not her fiancé who is shamed, but her own blindness" to the disparity between her pampered existence and that of the penurious shop-girl (the presumption duly rebounding on Betty).[17] In Geza von Bolvary's *Vagabond Queen* (1929), Balfour appears in double roles: as the put-upon skivvy in a Bloomsbury boarding house (as in *Cinders* [1927]), and as the Ruritanian Princess Zonia of Bolonia (ensconced at the Coronia in Mayfair) for whom she is mistaken. In *The Sea Urchin*, Balfour starts out as an orphan, Fay Wynchebec (in Mary Pickford-style ringlets), the daughter of the black sheep of an old and wealthy Cornish family, duly saved from service to the owner of a Paris night club by Jack Trebarrow (the scion of an anciently feuding neighboring estate and an enthusiastic—but somewhat incompetent—amateur pilot), who nevertheless stows away with her across the channel (far below decks, in the hold, they convivially mime a supper, by way of a garden fork, pickaxe, and bucket, in clumsy imitation, perhaps, of Chaplin's *The Gold Rush* [1925]). Again, foreshadowing *Champagne*, Jack and Fay are rescued in *The Sea Urchin* by a rowing boat.

Additionally, there is much in *Champagne*'s narrative of topical interest, appealing to a general contemporary audience. Indeed, I would suggest that the American magnate Harry Gordon Selfridge, who both cultivated and found himself an object of media attention, provides something of a model for the father, the "Wall Street Magnate" of *Champagne*.[18] In 1927, Selfridge was in the news, having controversially acquired the British department store, Whiteley's, of Bayswater—the subject of debate, not least, in parliamentary discussions leading to the passing of the 1927 Cinematograph Act.[19] Cinema was not the only commercial concern under threat from American competition. Selfridge was, furthermore, a keen supporter of aviation, in 1909 displaying in his Oxford Street flagship shop the airplane in which Blériot had just crossed the channel, thereby staging the first in any number of attention-seeking publicity stunts. Aviatrix leathers (of the sort donned by Betty in *Champagne*,

Figure 3

before unbuttoning them to reveal unscathed pearls and silk stockings) were modeled on the roof of Selfridge's store. Both of Selfridge's "flying heiress" daughters were married in the 1920s to pilots, and their exploits in the air provided matter for press coverage. Newspapers in the 1920s avidly carried stories of aviators and aviatrices—especially following Charles Lindbergh's 1927 solo crossing of the Atlantic, from New York to Paris, with "Cupid," headlined in *Champagne*, duly "taking a leaf from Lindy," to the accompaniment of a photograph of Balfour in a newspaper mock-up: "Wall Street Magnate Again Defied by Headstrong Heiress Daughter" (fig. 3). The aviatrix Amelia Earhart crossed the Atlantic, as a passenger, in a monoplane fitted with floats like a seaplane, piloted by Wilmer Stultz, in June 1928.[20] "Flying the Atlantic?," Betty is asked as she kisses goodbye to her father's sinking plane and passes several suitcases into the lifeboat. "Oh dear no," she casually replies, "I just wanted to catch this boat." Her father is embarrassed by his daughter, learning at secondhand, from a newspaper, of her escapade.

Production Context

Champagne's failure to garner critical approval in 1928 was surprising, given the credentials of the production team and cast contracted by BIP. Eliot Stannard was a consummate professional and a leading British scenario writer, a "Master of Screen Technique," publishing commentary on his craft as well as practicing it.[21] He had generated the Squibs series for Pearson (from a character in a one-act play); for Hitchcock he had worked on *The Ring* and adapted *Easy Virtue* (from Noel Coward's stageplay) and *The Farmer's Wife* (from Eden Philpott's stageplay).[22] Hitchcock was, by 1927, the highest paid director in Britain, establishing himself as both a commercial and critical success.[23] In October 1927, the generally equitable *Manchester Guardian* critic, Caroline Lejeune, advised:

> The injury which the British studios have drawn to themselves by praise of bad and inefficient workmanship is almost incalculable . . . To do our kinema justice I think that all, or most of its faults are negative ones. It has not the harsh technique of Italy, nor the crudeness of Russia, nor the insatiability of France nor the heaviness of Germany, nor the vulgarity of the United States. It simply has nothing, neither character nor courage, neither commercial success, skill nor artistic sense. It has no big men and no big ideas . . . Strip the British kinema of its essentials and you will find . . . one director, Alfred Hitchcock—who can be relied upon and two—Maurice Elvey and Walter Summers—who can be expected to provide the audience with good things and four films, *The Ring, The Battles of the Coronel and Falkland Islands, Hindle Wakes* and *The Lodger*—which have quality enough to give them extra national fame.[24]

In more than one sense, Hitchcock was British cinema's biggest man in 1927, of whom great things were expected in the courageous promotion of British cinema abroad.

As Tom Ryall and Andrew Higson have noted, British International emerged as a result of quarrels amongst personnel

involved with British National, a company which had already
signed-up actors with "extra national" appeal (including Syd
Chaplin, cast with Balfour in *A Little Bit of Fluff* [Robbins and
Dryden, 1928]).[25] British National acquired the services of
Hitchcock, in advance of the announcement of the launch of BIP,
within weeks of the opening of parliamentary debates leading
to the passing of the Cinematograph Act in December 1927.

The Act was designed to boost British film production and
to protect British distribution and exhibition from American
dominance. The government's intervention was prompted by
cultural and economic concerns—to counter brash American
"vulgarity" on both counts. Exhibitors and renters themselves
knew that American films were supplied in sufficient quantity
to satisfy audience demand and that American films attracted
audiences. They complained that cinema, as an industry, by
means of the Act, became subject to regulation from which
other American commodities and business interests remained
free. Meanwhile, the ambitions of BIP to produce and market
material appealing to an "extra national" audience, rather
than a specifically British audience, is graphically conveyed
even in the logo fronting *Champagne*: the figure of Britannia
sits foreground of a rotating globe. *Champagne*, provisionally,
courts the perceived appeal of Americana.

An assumption that such endeavors generally failed has
proved prejudicial to subsequent appraisals. Kenton Bamford, in
his survey of 1920s British cinema, apparently takes for granted
Rachael Low's retrospective dismissal of the generality of British
output: "It was widely accepted at the time, and has been so ever
since, that few of the films made in England during the twenties
were any good."[26] Admittedly, he provides a quantity of
evidence gathered from the trade and general press in support of
his argument—that British cinema failed to appeal to a mass
audience—while saying relatively little of the films themselves.
For Bamford, the Pearson-Balfour collaborations are exceptions
proving the rule.[27] For sure, Balfour's popularity was sufficiently
guaranteed that it passed without comment (after *Squibs*,
audiences clamored for Betty's return): "Of the films in which
Miss Betty Balfour appears it is unnecessary to speak," gushed a

Figure 4

Daily Telegraph journalist in 1924, while the *Daily Mail* simultaneously included Balfour in a gallery of English lovelies launching a number of British Film Weeks.[28] Off-screen, Balfour's star status was confirmed and enhanced by her endorsement of a wide and varied range of products; *Picturegoer* in February 1924 carried Balfour in Squibs "riches" guise (fig. 4) on its Special

Figure 5

British Number cover (marking the first Film Week) while routinely carrying Balfour ads for Maison Lyons Chocolates, Kia-Ora and Grossmith's creams and powders.[29] Balfour proved herself exceptionally adept in pleasing "every class of audience." While being critical in general of a system that promoted stars rather than stories, Iris Barry, a founder member of the Film Society (dedicated to showcasing film as art), remained loyal to Betty: "she simply has bags of talent and is worth seeing every single time."[30] Balfour makes her entry in *Champagne* distinctly framed as the film's star, isolated in a narrow hatchway, beamishly smiling direct to camera and instantly recognizable despite the sooty-face she proceeds to powder (fig 5). The film is a vehicle for Balfour as the airplane is a vehicle for Betty. Hitchcock's presentation of Balfour in *Champagne*, a meeting of a director with a star in whom producers, critics and audiences invested, is crucial to concurrent debates and aspirations to combine commercial success with artistic achievement.

Furthermore, Balfour was not only voted "Top World Star" of 1924 in a British poll, but was also one of the few British stars to command a following abroad. Along with

Novello, she consistently appeared in lists of souvenir postcards offered for sale by French fan magazines in the 1920s, by whom she was also interviewed; a Betty Balfour film "cannot fail to please," claimed *Cinémagazine* in 1927.[31] For Louis Mercanton she filmed the society comedy *Monte Carlo* (1925) and for Marcel L'Herbier appeared as the tragic heroine of a story of Normandy Fisher Folk, *Little Devil May Care* (*Le Diable au Coeur*, 1927). Her presence in Nice for the filming of various scenes for Mercanton's *Cinders* (*La Petite Bonne du Palace*) was acknowledged by the May 1926 front cover of *Ciné-Théatre de la Côte d'Azur*. Writing for the art journal *The Studio*, Robert Herring (another Film Society stalwart) praised L'Herbier's direction, saying that he had drawn from his star a performance which no British director had as yet managed to discover.[32]

Balfour's range spanned the family melodrama and comedy of the Squibs series to the drama and romantic comedy of *The Sea Urchin*, *Champagne,* and *Bright Eyes*. In *Champagne*, accosted by the Boy (who has returned with the Father) at the foot of the stairs at the cabaret (and blocking the progress of a waiter who distractingly makes several attempts to get past the arguing threesome), Betty is momentarily accorded a blank background against which she expresses a gamut of emotions (she insists that she was only trying to help when the Father accuses her of disgracing him; then she is amused; then upset) before, realizing her humiliation, dashing away. In her performances, Balfour displayed an affective command of both pathos (the orphanage's "little mother" of *The Sea Urchin* and Jenny's more harsh casting out onto the street in *Bright Eyes*) and "low" comedy (slapstick): sentiments appealing to a wide, popular audience.[33] *Champagne* ends with Betty crossing her eyeballs and a ship's waiter intervening in the tussle between Man and Boy; *Bright Eyes* ends with Jenny unceremoniously plonked down on her own birthday cake as Jean proposes marriage: "Bet your little dickey on that," she says. Furthermore, the score for the sound version of *Bright Eyes* carries a personalized theme (sometimes sung by Balfour herself), underscoring (as do lyrics in the sound version of *Blackmail*) the blonde's sex appeal —

> Oh my word
> Isn't she a bird
> She's got It and lots of It
> And that ain't all

—duly applauded in the film's sound effects. Mirror shots in *Champagne* and *Bright Eyes* display Balfour's cropped blonde mane and bare back. Typically, in both films, Balfour is presented as both dowdy duckling and glamorous swan. In *Bright Eyes*, Jenny is dumbfounded when she first confronts her own reflection, then marvels at the transformation that Lola's gown, tiara, and silk stockings have effected on her appearance.

The Sea Urchin and *Champagne* provide Balfour with ample opportunity for comic business. In the former, domestic fixtures and fittings (bath-sheets, chairs, carpets) collectively participate in the action, threatening/promising to effect Fay's disrobement and further embarrassments. Crucially, Balfour excelled at visual comedy (including *Champagne*'s battles with pastry and a mattress) and in delivering vitality and apparent spontaneity in exuberantly expressive performances (in *Champagne* this repeatedly and characteristically takes the form of a mocking defiance of adverse circumstances and reversals of fortune, with disappointment or despair soon giving way to smiling optimism). She playfully twiddles her thumbs when Jean produces his ring to mark their engagement; after the initial reeling shock of the Father's declaration of bankruptcy, Betty looks askance and nudges towards him as though she does not take what he has said entirely seriously.

Balfour had drawing power. Although she may not have achieved the superstar status enjoyed by Pickford, her casting by BIP in the late 1920s, as an internationally recognized figure, was as important to the company's ambitions and marketing strategy as the hiring of the American Chinese actress Anna May Wong for *Piccadilly* and of the Russian actress (by way of Germany) Olga Chekhova, alongside Jean

Bradin, for *Moulin Rouge* (E.A. Dupont, 1928).[34] The British actor Jack Trevor, Balfour's co-star in *Bright Eyes*, built his career in Germany and was cast and promoted in terms of his transnational appeal.[35] However, beyond *Champagne's* pairing of an internationally recognized star with an internationally regarded director, there are other aspects of *Champagne* that might have augured better for the film's immediate reception.

The Sea Urchin, Champagne, and *Bright Eyes* make good use of character types and readily identifiable character actors: Clifford Heatherley reprises his performance as Sullivan, the smarmy cabaret manager masquerading as Fay's father in *The Sea Urchin*, for the oleaginous *maître d'* in *Champagne*, rubbing his hands, curling his waxed moustache, and puffing out his chest, as occasion demands; Gordon Harker, who appeared as a fairground boxing tout in *The Ring* and as the hung-lipped, curmudgeonly old retainer Churdles Ash in *The Farmer's Wife*, hams magnificently as the cigar-chewing magnate in *Champagne* (he chews even while he exercises). Jean, in *Bright Eyes*, starts out as a gigolo (but fancies himself as something better). A bustling concierge (as in Cutts's *The Blackguard* [1925] and in *Blackmail*) and a haughty, sneering, French *doméstique* are amongst *Champagne's* typical roles, again calling for visually recognizable, characteristically demonstrative performances.

Tim Bergfelder has justifiably commented upon the frequency with which popular films of the 1920s convey transnational travel by way of their scenarios.[36] Whereas *The Sea Urchin*, figuratively, takes the audience across the channel, *Champagne*, referentially, crosses the Atlantic. The action of *Downhill* and *Easy Virtue* moves from England to the South of France and back again. Hitchcock's production design for Cutts's *The Blackguard* attempts unconvincingly to convey a Russian setting for part of the action, as fantastical as Raymond Paton's conception in his original novel.[37] *Bright Eyes*, on the other hand, evokes a more generalized notion of the modern, cosmopolitan, continental city, with a black jazz band accompanying fancy toe-tapping and sparky hoofing on the dance floor: the setting of this story is indeterminate, as it could equally be London or Berlin or

Paris (where *Bright Eyes* is set) or even Vienna (where the film was, incidentally, actually shot). Bergfelder likewise draws attention to the recurrence of particular forms of spectacular entertainment incorporated into the films pitched at an international audience: circuses, variety halls, night clubs, cabarets; the action of *The Ring* covers a fairground and boxing. Dancing, as spectacle and as commonplace activity, featured in British film production before and alongside the purposeful European ventures of the later 1920s.[38] Hitchcock's *The Pleasure Garden* launches itself into dance in its credits sequence; *The Ring* features a Charleston. Lola dances a tango in *Bright Eyes* in addition to Balfour's "Squibs" number. *A Little Bit of Fluff* combined Balfour with the Plaza Tiller Girls while Jack Buchanan appeared, effectively, as himself in Cutts's *Confetti* (1927). Chili Bouchier was similarly cast in Maurice Elvey's *Palais de Danse* (1928) and Anthony Asquith's *Shooting Stars* (1928), while a Chili Bouchier look-alike (Sunday Wilshin) appears in *Champagne's* cabaret scenes. *The Blackguard* imitates Cossack dancing, in an attempt to authenticate its staged settings (as does *The Sea Urchin*, as exotic entertainment, in an equally staged Paris). Cutts's Rat series offers a variety of dance styles, with *The Rat* (1925) delivering a fox-trot ("the Rat step") and *The Triumph of the Rat* (1926) adding Isadora Duncan-style "Greek" dancing. Novello, as Cutts's eponymous "Rat," plays an apache while *The Sea Urchin* includes an extensive, vigorously dramatic and gymnastic interlude of apache-style dancing, as sensation and sub-text: this offers something of a model for the cabaret sequence in *Champagne* where a female dancer suddenly dives from an upper gallery, to be caught by her equally athletic male partner below. The dancing couple spin around and Betty's mind is in a whirl. Into whose hands will Betty be safely thrown? In whom can Betty trust? Christine Gledhill, reporting contemporary critics, identifies sensational interventions as typical of Cutts's repertoire.[39] Meanwhile, *Champagne* mocks more humdrum, participatory, dancing: huddled couples on the cabaret dance floor, mismatched partners, are likened to an interjected shot of huddled sheep.

Figure 6

The opportunity granted by dancing to expose areas of flesh as an attraction was much spoken of by both British and continental critics in the 1920s. The bare legs of girls in netball knickers were displayed in *Alley Cat*; in *Champagne* a dancer on the ship swirls, spinning her dress, to expose her legs.[40] Indeed, legs are featured throughout *Champagne*, with the theatrical agent's assistant curiously lifting Betty's skirt, with an extended polished shoe, before deciding that her legs are a marketable proposition. Betty's introduction to the Paris cabaret is staged by way of a point of view shot of a line of women's legs hanging from bar stools (the women's male companions are subsequently revealed). In *Bright Eyes*, there is an under-the-table shot of diamante-heeled shoes and silk-stockinged legs crossing in eager anticipation of favors the millionaire may choose to bestow on the selected companion from a line of contenders vying for attention. *Champagne* emphatically and explicitly stages its display of bodies as a diverting, spectacular attraction: the Boy and the Girl, the romantic couple, constituting an item of narrative interest, are thrown into shadow, foreground, while behind them, a scantily clad, sequined, gyrating cabaret dancer is spotlit (fig. 6). There is here, too, an "oscillation" of tone within a single frame, a technique inherited from *The Pleasure Garden* and *Downhill*. A similarly awkward, uneasy disjuncture occurs at the end of *The 39 Steps*, with Mr. Memory resolving the suspense by dramatically reciting the secret betraying the band of spies pursued by Richard Hannay, and a highly illuminated, high-kicking chorus line meanwhile distracting attention to the background: the show must go on.

Production design contributes much to the spectacular appeal of *Champagne*, a feature shared with many of the circus and cabaret settings of the 1920s. The dance halls of *The Pleasure Garden* and *Downhill* are indicative of a broader trend. In 1927, Sinclair Hill's *A Woman Redeemed* was hailed for the most extravagant set yet constructed in a British studio: girls in swimming costumes dive, Busby Berkeley style, from a rising multi-tiered platform into a pool of water in an ersatz Paris night club.[41] Walter Murton's set was possibly trumped at the end of the decade by Andrew Mazzei's Art Deco set for Maurice Elvey's *High Treason* (1929) and by Alfred Junge for *Piccadilly*, again combining choreography with large and lavish sets. Frequently, set design and cinematography are mutually enhancing. For *The Lodger*, Hitchcock required a four-storied staircase, as in *Blackmail*, purposefully, literally, heightening suspense.[42] For *Champagne*, C.W. Arnold, Hitchcock's companion as set designer on *The Lodger*, *Blackmail*, and *Rich and Strange* (and Cutts's designer for *The Sea Urchin*), built a decoratively stenciled and fret-worked, double-galleried cabaret set, shown off to full advantage by Jack Cox (another regular Hitchcock collaborator) in a 360-degree panning shot.

Sometimes cinematography in *Champagne* provides an attraction in itself. Among other *tour de force* technical flourishes (dissolves and multiple overlays), Barr rates the film's framing shots of the Man's point of view through the bottom of a champagne glass: it "must have been extremely complicated to set up, involving a giant champagne glass and possibly a special lens and a lot of trial and error."[43] The Boy, seasick and in bed, removes a cloth from his head and sees Betty in triplicate: one image sways to the left and its reverse sways to the right, with a central close-up meanwhile lunging

Figure 7

towards him (fig. 7). In the manner of *The Sea Urchin*, a traveling camera follows Betty as she stoops in her garret to pick up a glinting dropped knife and (via overlays) one wonders whether she intends to wield this against the petulant Boy or the predatory Man (perhaps a preparatory exercise for *Blackmail*).[44] Indeed, as Kelly Robinson has observed, cinematography was recognized widely by British producers as a means of creating spectacle, and *Champagne*'s cinematography was praised by contemporary critics as one of its significant achievements.[45]

As is well-known, German cinematography was generally admired in the 1920s. Hence, the hiring of German cinematographers for productions aiming at an international market was recognized as a promotional asset.[46] Theodor Sparkhul (who had worked with director Dupont and cinematographer Werner Brandes in Germany, and with director Cutts and designer Hitchcock on *The Blackguard*) was appointed for *Bright Eyes*. Here "technical flourishes" include the double exposure sequence in which Jenny imagines Jean with a bouquet of roses, arriving at the garret to share her forlorn birthday supper and purloined champagne. Sparkhul went on to assist Brandes on *The Informer* (Arthur Robison, 1929), made, like *Champagne, Bright Eyes, Moulin Rouge,* and *Piccadilly,* for BIP.

British imitation of the example set by German studios, in both set design and cinematography, could be considered as the highest form of flattery. There is evidence that both Hitchcock (partly through his work in Germany on *The Pleasure Garden*) and Asquith (in, for instance, *Shooting Stars*) viewed German films shown at the Film Society and more widely, in regular venues, through distribution agreements secured with continental distributors.[47] However, the importation of "foreign" style into British cinema was not unanimously well-received in Britain. Flattery by imitation could play both in favor of and against British producers. This accounts, in part, for the lukewarm reception of *Champagne* in 1928, despite its combination of elements intended to pitch it for popular and critical success.

Reception Climate

In August 1929, *The Architectural Review* (which frequently published articles by contributors to the high-brow journal *Close Up* and by other members of the Film Society), delivered an enthusiastic appraisal of the sound version of Hitchcock's *Blackmail*, "The Best Talking Film Yet—and British":

[From an] essentially familiar basis, the tragic theme is developed with a high degree of artistic skill. From its beginning to its end the film is filled with the insistent note of doom. . . . We may say, without hesitation, that the synchronised sound and speech, as they are used in this film, have not only a definite value in drawing out the dramatic content of the film, but that they have become, in fact, integral to its structure. . . . Mr. Hitchcock has shown the same discernment in the selection of the aural image as we have learnt to expect from him in the choice of the visual image. Just as, in the silent film, only those images are depicted which have a significant bearing on the content of the film, so here, also, only those sounds are heard which have a definite part to play in the development of the tale or theme.[48]

In its tone of condescension and surprise, the appraisal is symptomatic of the stance usually adopted by these journals towards British cinema. Moreover, this clique of "high-brow" reviewers was remarkable for the indulgence it allowed itself in the contradiction of its own critical parameters. While European technical expertise was repeatedly presented to British producers and directors as a standard for emulation, those same producers and directors could find themselves lambasted for striving too hard, too overtly, in their pursuit of European models. Again, the *Blackmail* review is indicative of a routine reservation that technique should be placed in the service of the story: that spectacle for its own sake should not be allowed to subsume or substitute for the exposition of character and narrative. *Moulin Rouge* and *Piccadilly* (similarly triangulated and squared love stories), along with *Champagne*, were criticized for negligible plot value, for which spectacular appeal failed to compensate.[49] One might suggest that a standing record of delivery and expectation, acknowledged in the later *Blackmail* review, counted against Hitchcock in the disappointing reception of *Champagne* (he had set his own bar high). The story was, apparently, the thing, beyond spectacle and stars. Hitchcock duly realigned himself with this strand of 1920s criticism in subsequent interviews.

Furthermore, I suggest, *Champagne* was caught in an additional bind, more generally expressed, by dint of its release in the wake of debates leading to the passing of the 1927 Cinematograph Act. In other words, statutory intervention carried consequences for both the film's production context and its climate of reception—in Britain. As is well-known, the Act was largely prompted by concerns that American films advertised and promoted American manners and mores to British and British Empire audiences. The trade paper *Kine Weekly* said that *Champagne* had a "distinct pseudo-American flavour" and that it was "a feeble imitation of the type of entertainment at which the Americans are unsurpassed."[50] Schematically speaking, British films were as readily criticized for shadowing popularist (supposedly) American content as for following (supposedly) European style. While one consequence of the debates was the establishment of international links in production and distribution, another was a widespread call for a specifically British cinema. Women, who constituted the larger part of the cinema-going audience, were addressed as a matter of particular concern— notoriously, as "temporary American citizens":

> The plain truth about the film situation is that the bulk of our picture-goers are Americanised to the extent that makes them regard a British film as a foreign film and an interesting but more frequently an irritating interlude in their favourite entertainment. They go to see American stars; they have been brought up on American publicity. They talk America, think American and dream America.[51]

Thus, while Asquith's *Shooting Stars* provides reflexive commentary on the concurrent relationship between Britain and America at the level of industrial production (with British talent launched to international fame in Hollywood), the critical reception of *Champagne* reflects concurrent British attitudes towards the promotion of American-style consumerism, not least through cinema.[52] *Champagne*, while ostensibly courting the appeal of Americana, was released in the wake of a parliamentary chorus of disapproval of Americanization. Betty, as the spoilt heiress (possibly a surrogate for the daughter of a department store magnate) is chastised for her conspicuous, extravagant, consumption but resourcefully adapts herself to reduced circumstances. Furthermore, *Champagne* acerbically debases and debunks the superficiality of the glamour on which the rich and privileged waste their wealth. *Champagne*'s lure for audiences, on the other hand, was assumed to lie precisely in its display of these luxuries, despite its blatant criticism of their consumption. However vicariously, the film allowed young women to enjoy a magical sense of abandon in sharing a slice of the heiress life—albeit qualified by a thudding reminder of all-too-familiar pressing concerns—in Britain, as elsewhere. *Champagne* temporarily delivered an escape by airplane and ocean liner (no less) to a world of frenetic dancing, snappy gowns, and knock-out cocktails. Not least amongst *Champagne*'s attractions was Betty Balfour herself, as a vivacious character and star in whom audiences emotionally invested. In *Champagne*, Betty proves herself resilient in the face of hardship, determined to earn her own keep. Yet in attempting to please a wide audience—an attempt to reconcile "art" with "commerce"—*Champagne* simultaneously fell foul of a number of particular, vested, critical agendas.

Conclusion

Viewing *Champagne* in retrospect, there is in many of its "technical flourishes" evidence of experimentation to which Hitchcock would subsequently return. However, these flourishes frequently serve not merely as attractions, calling for attention, but, as in *The Lodger* and *Blackmail*, to charge "the screen rectangle with emotion," serving the story rather than, as Durgnat seemed to suggest, doing nothing.[53]

In addition to locating *Champagne* in a Hitchcockian landscape, it has seemed worth discussing the film in a broader context of national and international production, distribution and exhibition. *Champagne* is, I suggest, a porous text. On the one hand, it absorbs spectacular and story material from *The Sea Urchin*, sharing personnel in front of and behind the camera. *Bright Eyes* even opens with an apparently conscious reference to the earlier film: "given the choice," reads an intertitle, "Jenny would have preferred to be a millionaire," as we find Balfour cheerily washing glasses in the sill-room. *Champagne* marks continuities in the exploitation of Balfour's talents as an actor and of Balfour's established personae on and off screen.

There is much to be celebrated in *Champagne*. Betty is portrayed as a modern girl, determined to earn her keep (and to keep her father) when the need arises. Hitchcock sympathetically accords Betty her dignity even while setting her up as the butt of her father's humiliating hoax. Betty is both the object of her father's censure and correction, and subjectively independent and resourceful. Despite Maurice Yacowar's dismissal of the film's plot as merely a series of "false alarms," *Champagne* amply supports his observation that, even in Hitchcock's early work, "smug security is upset by the revelation of disorder," with Betty deprived of her security both in parental approval and in her lover's trustworthiness.[54] More broadly, the smug security of Betty's leisured class of friends is revealed to be sham, and even their friendship may be no more than superficial; the lover is tested to prove himself worthy of her love. As in *Bright Eyes*, accidental disruptions of social status are used pointedly to comment upon social snobbery. *Champagne* does more with its use of newspaper headlines than advance the narrative: it jibes at salacious media fascination with scandals attending the rich and famous. Contemporary critics, I suggest, responded to *Champagne*'s necessary display of luxury rather than to the bilious critique of conspicuous consumption it afforded.

There is more irony in *Champagne* than previous commentary has acknowledged, effected by connective titling and, especially, in Balfour's performance as Betty. The film owes as much to Balfour as it does to Hitchcock. Moreover, an oscillation between suspense and comedy, however trickily handled and uneasily conveyed by Balfour in *Champagne*, may be regarded as typical of Hitchcock, within a frame, within a film, and across the canon.

There is a moral to the tale here told. Neither star status (on the part of Balfour) nor received recognition (on the part of Hitchcock and Stannard), nor its ambitious *mise-en-scène* and spectacular entertainment value, could guarantee *Champagne* even moderate, let alone widespread, success at the time of its release. It seems worth studying the film in the context of 1920s debates concerning issues of production and reception in order to understand the sometimes conflicting criteria against which it was measured. Its engagement with topical events and a popular demand for particular stars make *Champagne* very much a film of its time but also one which merits reappraisal—regardless of Hitchcock's own retrospective poor opinion of its status. Rather than dismissing *Champagne* as an aberration in Hitchcock's career, we might choose, more usefully, to regard the film as operating within the exigencies, the shifting sands, of more general contemporaneous and ongoing critical appraisal of Hitchcock and his relationship with British silent cinema.

Notes

With special thanks to Stephen Horne, Alain Kerzoncuf, and Charles Barr; also thanks to Kelly Robinson, Pamela Hutchinson, and especially to Sid Gottlieb for their comments on the first draft of this paper, and to Kathleen Dickson and Steve Tollervey, BFI Viewing Services.

1. The Southbank screening was simultaneously streamed live. The BFI National Archive copy of *Champagne*, before and after restoration (on which this essay relies), differs significantly from the DVD distributed by Optimum as an item in its *Early Hitchcock Collection* (2007). The restored version opens with a champagne cork popping and the view of the dance hall through the bottom of a glass; it makes sense of the imagined assault; and also of the closing chase sequence.

2. Charles Barr, *English Hitchcock* (Moffat: Cameron and Hollis, 1999), 62; John Russell Taylor, *Hitch: The Life and Work of Alfred Hitchcock* (London: Faber and Faber, 1978), 93. See also, Sidney Gottlieb, "Hitchcock's Silent Cinema," in Thomas Leitch and Leland Poague, eds., *A Companion to Alfred Hitchcock* (Chichester: Wiley Blackwell, 2011), 255-69.

3. François Truffaut, *Hitchcock* (London: Secker and Warburg, 1968), 47. As the centenary BiFi exhibition in Paris demonstrated, Truffaut courted Hitchcock assiduously and Hitch was correspondingly flattered by his attention. For a more appreciative

summary from France, see Eric Rohmer and Claude Chabrol, *Hitchcock*, translated by Stanley Hochman (New York: Frederick Ungar, 1979), 16-17.

4. Michael Powell, *A Life in Movies* (London: Heinemann, 1986), 185.

5. Raymond Durgnat, *The Strange Case of Alfred Hitchcock* (London: Faber and Faber, 1974), 83. For *Champagne* as a "much-maligned" film with remarkable things in it, while falling flat, see William Rothman, *Hitchcock—The Murderous Gaze* (Cambridge: Harvard University Press, 1982), 353.

6. Tom Ryall, *Alfred Hitchcock and the British Cinema* (1986; rpt. London: Athlone, 1996), 21. For Ryall's qualifications of this view, see his *Anthony Asquith* (Manchester: Manchester University Press, 2005), 34-43.

7. See Tania Modleski's *The Women Who Knew Too Much* (New York and London: Routledge, 1988); Ryall's *Blackmail* (London: BFI, 1993); Michael Walker, *Hitchcock's Motifs* (Amsterdam: Amsterdam University Press, 2005); in addition to Matthias Müller's compilations, shown at the 1999 exhibition, *Notorious: Hitchcock and Contemporary Art* (MOMA, Oxford) and cited by Erika Balsom, "The Hitchcock of Contemporary Art," *Hitchcock Annual* 17 (2011): 129-67.

8. Both Barr, *English Hitchcock*, 223-24, and Durgnat, *The Strange Case of Alfred Hitchcock,* 83, recognize "Theo von Alten" as Ferdinand von Alten, active in German films of the 1920s. A "younger woman on the make" had previously appeared in *The Pleasure Garden* (1926).

9. "*Champagne,*" *The Bioscope*, 22 August 1928, 929; see also Hugh Castle's review, "Some British Films," in the high-brow journal *Close Up*, July 1929, dismissing the film as "champagne that had been left in the rain all night"; and Kenton Bamford's summary of a more positive popular response in *Distorted Images: British National Identity and Film in the 1920's* (London: I.B. Tauris, 1999), 146-47.

10. A.J. Hitchcock, "Titles—Artistic and Otherwise," *The Motion Picture Studio*, 21 July 1921, 6.

11. See *Close Up*, August 1928, for complaints regarding occasionally laborious mannerisms in *The Ring*: "Well, it *is* treated visually, but then its merit ends. Mr Hitchcock's method is to depict one simple fact, that a sub-title could have got over, by a long sequence, or a number of elaborate tricks . . . the time and expense were out of proportion to the effect." See also Rachael Low, *The*

History of the British Film IV (1971; rpt. London: Routledge, 1997), 237. *The Ring* was, on the other hand, enthusiastically received by *Picturegoer.*

12. A similar maneuver is used by Hitchcock in *The Skin Game* (1931): from a fondly familiar point of view shot of a country estate, the camera pulls back to reveal the same shot featured on a poster announcing the public auction of this parkland, ripe for commercial development and exploitation.

13. Taylor, *Hitch*, 93. Mycroft reported on film matters for London's *Evening Standard* and was also a member of the Film Society. Maurice Yacowar, in *Hitchcock's British Films* (Hamden: Archon Books, 1977), 77-78, further reports Hitchcock as saying that *Champagne* "ended up with a hodge-podge of a story that was written as we went through the film and I thought it was dreadful." Yacowar dismisses *Champagne* as the worst feature Hitchcock ever made.

14. See Amy Sargeant, "Night and Fog and Benighted Ladies," *Adaptation* 3, no. 1 (2009): 36-51, for a discussion of this recurrent topography in films of the 1920s.

15. On the commodification of Josephine Baker in Paris in the 1920s, see, for instance, Christopher Wilk *et al.*, *Modernism: Designing a New World* (London: V & A Publishing, 2006).

16. Titles to *Squibs' Honeymoon*, cited by Amy Sargeant, *British Cinema: A Critical History* (London: BFI, 2005), 94.

17. Christine Gledhill, *Reframing British Cinema 1918-1928: Between Restraint and Passion* (London: BFI, 2003), 141.

18. The producer and director, Victor Saville, befriended Selfridge: his *Love on Wheels* (1933) is, effectively, a feature-length advertisement for Selfrdge's Oxford Street store, confirming Selfridge's appetite for publicity.

19. See *Parliamentary Debates: Commons* (London: HMSO, 1927) v. 203, and Kathryn A. Morrison, *English Shops and Shopping: An Architectural History* (New Haven: Yale University Press, 2003), 137. Lawrence Napper, in *British Cinema and Middlebrow Culture in the Interwar Years* (Exeter: University of Exeter Press, 2009), 31, notes that the book trade likewise complained that the film industry was to receive unfair protection.

20. Lady Heath and Stella Wolfe Murray, *Woman and Flying* (London: John Long, 1929), 221. The journalist, Wolfe Murray, comments disparagingly on media coverage of Earhart as merely a "passenger." In *The Sea Urchin*, Trebarrow's craft, "Windy Willie," is

delivered ground-bound and in parsimonious balsa wood model shots, with a stock aerial view of the Panthéon and the Luxembourg Gardens (I think) marking Trebarrow's arrival in Paris.

21. For discussion of Stannard's articles and 1920 manual, see Charles Barr, "Writing Screen Plays: Stannard and Hitchcock," in Andrew Higson, ed., *Young and Innocent? The Cinema in Britain 1896-1930* (Exeter: University of Exeter Press, 2002), 227-41; also Gerry Turvey, "Enter the Intellectuals: Eliot Stannard, Harold Weston and the Discourse on Cinema and Art," 85-93, and Michael Eaton, "Hitch and Strange," 110-17, reciting Stannard's four fundamental rules— Sybolism, Atmosphere, Continuity, (and, most importantly) Theme— in Alan Burton and Laraine Porter, eds., *Scene-Stealing: Sources for British Cinema Before 1930* (Trowbridge: Flicks Books, 2003).

22. I have reservations about *Easy Virtue*, to be pursued on another occasion: not least of which is that Stannard betrays the back story at the outset rather than (as does Coward) withholding it. Suspense, for the film's audience, lies in the anticipation of the mother-in-law's discovery of Larita's secret, while the father-in-law continues to support Larita, regardless of her "shaming" divorce.

23. See Ryall, *Alfred Hitchcock and the British Cinema*, 91-92.

24. Caroline Lejeune, "Cinema," *Manchester Guardian*, 8 October 1927, 11.

25. Ryall, *Alfred Hitchcock and the British Cinema*, 46-47; Andrew Higson, "Polyglot Films for an International Market: E.A. Dupont, the British Film Industry, and the Idea of a European Cinema, 1926-1930," in Andrew Higson and Richard Maltby, eds., *Film Europe and Film America* (Exeter: University of Exeter Press, 1999), 274-301, at 279.

26. Low, *The History of the British Film*, IV, 157-58; compare Bamford, *Distorted Images*, 120, offering one evaluation of what "good" might mean for a mass audience.

27. Bamford, *Distorted Images*, 88, 137, 158-59.

28. Alder Anderson, "All-British Film Week: Bid for National Patronage," *Daily Telegraph*, 4 February 1924, 6, and *Daily Mail*, 4 February 1924, 1; see also *Picturegoer*, February 1924, 12-13, for Kinema Club Carnival, with stars arriving at the Hotel Cecil, London, in costumes from recent roles. For a discussion of Balfour's popularity and especially of her first collaboration with Pearson, *Nothing Else Matters* (1920), see Judith McLaren, " 'My career up to now': Betty Balfour and the Background to the Squibs Series," in Alan Burton and Laraine Porter, eds., *Pimple, Pranks and Pratfalls:*

British Film Comedy Before 1930 (Trowbridge: Flicks Books, 2000), 76-81. Balfour had appeared for Fred Karno and, when only eleven, in a solo revue sketch for C.B. Cochran (possibly the source for her skivvy dance in *Bright Eyes*). She was spotted by Welsh, of Welsh-Pearson, while working for Cochran, then, when performing at the Alhambra, received the offer of her first film with the company.

29. Bamford, *Distorted Images,* 142, and *Picturegoer*, October 1923 and October 1924; also July, August, and October 1925 numbers for Kia Ora ads, and January 1929 for Grossmith's. English lovely Ivy Duke also promoted Pond's Cold Cream, while equally lovely Edna Best endorsed Eastern Foam vanishing cream.

30. Iris Barry, *Let's Go to the Pictures* (London: Chatto and Windus, 1926), 120.

31. *Cinémagazine,* 30 September 1927, 589; see also, "Travaille-t-on en Angleterre? Betty Balfour va nous le dire," *Ciné-Miroir*, 3 May 1929, 282, for usual autobiographical material and Balfour's timely comments on the pressing need to promote British cinema in the Dominions. Typically, the article is accompanied by both a glamourous, autographed portrait shot (Betty with bare shoulders, pearls, and feathers, looking up to the camera) and a more menial, everyday rendition (Betty in *Little Devil May Care*). For more on the reception of Balfour in France, see Amy Sargeant *"Everyone's Doing the Riviera* Because *It's So Much Nicer in Nice,"* in Laraine Porter and Bryony Dixon, eds., *Picture Perfect* (Exeter: Exeter Press, 2007), 92-103; for an appraisal of the transatlantic exportability of Novello and Balfour, see Bamford, *Distorted Images*, 96.

32. Robert Herring, "The Cinema," *The Studio*, 96 (1928), 99.

33. See McLaren, " 'My career up to now,' " p. 78, for an appreciation of Balfour's talents in pathos and low comedy.

34. *Piccadilly* also, of course, cast the Ziegfeld Follies dancer Gilda Gray as Mabel; for confirmation of Gray's celebrity, see F. Scott Fitzgerald, *Trimalchio: An Early Version of The Great Gatsby* (originally written in 1924; Cambridge: Cambridge University Press, 2000), 34.

35. See "Continental Britons," *Picturegoer*, March 1929, for comments on Lilian Harvey, "stranded in Germany," alongside Warwick Ward and Vivian Gibson. While some British actors occasionally appeared in continental collaborations (for instance, Warwick Ward in Arthur Robison's 1928 *Looping the Loop* [*Die Todesschleife*], Henry Edwards in Steinhoff's 1928 *Fear* [*Angst*] and Guy Newall in Geza von Bolvary's *Number Seventeen* [1929]), Jack Trevor was unusual in choosing to build a career abroad (see, for

instance, his performances for Michael Curtiz, as a suave French con-man in the delightful *Fiaker Nr.13* [1926] and as a Cambridge undergraduate in *The Golden Butterfly* [1926], in addition to a composer falsely suspected of murder in *Alley Cat*). Trevor's son, Robert Steane, appears in Tacita Dean's film *Boots* (2003) and tells something of his father's story.

36. Tim Bergfelder, "Negotiating Exoticism: Hollywood, Film Europe and the Cultural Reception of Anna May Wong," in Higson and Maltby, *Film Europe and Film America*, 302-24, at 303. Erich von Stroheim's *Foolish Wives* (1922), set on the fashionable Riviera, managed to convey travel by way of enormous Hollywood studio sets.

37. For commentary on Paton's 1923 novel, *The Autobiography of a Blackguard*, and Cutts's film, see Amy Sargeant, "Good and Bad Russians: Russians in British Literature and Film between the Wars," paper given at Russia Abroad conference, Moscow, 2008.

38. See Sargeant, *British Cinema*, 96; also Cathy Ross, *Twenties London: A City in the Jazz Age* (London: Philip Wilson Publishers Ltd., 2003), for various representations of jazz and jazz dancing.

39. Gledhill, *Reframing British Cinema 1918-1928*, 113-14.

40. For German commentary on *Alley Cat*, see Sargeant, "Night and Fog."

41. See New Era press book for *A Woman Redeemed* and Sargeant, "The Return of Mata Hari: *A Woman Redeemed* (Sinclair Hill, 1927)," *Historical Journal of Radio, Film and Television* 30, no. 1 (2010): 37-54.

42. Ryall, *Alfred Hitchcock and the British Cinema*, 25; Ryall, *Blackmail*, 26 and 44-45. It is worth noting also, as reinforcement of German influence on Hitchcock, the London sequence in Pabst's *Pandora's Box* (1928).

43. Barr, *English Hitchcock*, 64.

44. Gledhill, *Reframing British Cinema 1918-1928*, 116.

45. *The Bioscope*, 22 August 1928, 929; Kelly Robinson, "Flamboyant Realism: Werner Brandes and British International Pictures in the Late 1920s," in Tim Bergfelder and Christian Cargnelli, eds., *Destination London: German-Speaking Emigrés and British Cinema 1925-1950* (New York: Berghahn, 2008), 62-77, at 62; also Robinson's unpublished Ph.D. thesis, "British International Pictures and the Influence of German Cinematographers, 1927-1936," University of Southampton, 2008, 160, on *Kinematograph Weekly*'s praise and acknowledgement of Sparkhul's photography of *Bright Eyes* as a "selling point." See also Sidney Gottlieb, "Early Hitchcock: The German Influence," *Hitchcock Annual* 8 (1999-2000): 100-30.

46. As Robinson, in "Flamboyant Realism," 63, comments, it was additionally a practical necessity; see also David Cunynghame diaries, BFI Special Collections.

47. See Ryall, *Alfred Hitchcock and the British Cinema*, 63, on Fritz Lang's *Die Nibelungen* (1924); also Joseph Garncarz, "German Hitchcock," *Hitchcock Annual* 9 (2000-2001): 73-99. *Die Nibelungen* was also screened at the Royal Albert Hall (as was Cutts's *The Blackguard*), in a gala performance with a Wagnerian prologue and sub-Wagnerian accompaniment played by the London Symphony Orchestra; it ran for some forty screenings, from April to June 1924. *Faust* was shown in 1927; see Royal Albert Hall programs, 28 April 1924 and 20 April 1925. Naomi Mitchison, sister of J.B.S. Haldane, a founding member of the Film Society, recalled seeing *Die Nibelungen* at the Royal Albert Hall; see *You May Well Ask: A Memoir 1920-1940* (London: Victor Gollancz, 1979), 40; see also, *Picturegoer*, December 1926, 50.

48. "Mercurius," "The Best Talking Film Yet—and British," *The Architectural Review*, August 1929, 87; see also Ryall, *Blackmail*, 25-30, for the reception of *Blackmail* in general, trade, and minority film culture press.

49. Regarding *Moulin Rouge*, see Robinson, "Flamboyant Realism," 72, and Higson, "Polyglot Films for an International Market," 281. For comparable German complaints about *Piccadilly*, see Sargeant, "Night and Fog."

50. See Bamford, *Distorted Images*, 147.

51. *Daily Express*, 18 March 1927, quoted in *Parliamentary Debates*, 204.

52. For the context of *Shooting Stars*, see Gledhill, *Reframing British Cinema 1918-1928*, 149-50, and Sargeant, *British Cinema*, 102-03.

53. See Truffaut, *Hitchcock*, 50.

54. See Yacowar, *Hitchcock's British Films*, 12.

CHARLES BARR

Hitchcock and Documentary: Re-Editing Men of the Lightship

The two short narratives that Hitchcock directed in 1944 about the French Resistance, *Bon Voyage* and *Aventure Malgache*, are now reasonably well known and available.[1] He had travelled from Hollywood to England in response to an appeal by Sidney Bernstein, a powerful figure in the Films Division of the British Ministry of Information (MoI).[2] The two men, born within a few months of each other in 1899, had been friends since the 1920s, when Hitchcock was at the start of his directing career and Bernstein was a dynamic young impresario; at the end of the war they would jointly form the independent company Transatlantic, fated never fully to recover from the failure of its second production, *Under Capricorn* (1949).

Those two French Resistance films were not, however, the first work that Hitchcock had done for Bernstein and the Films Division. Patrick McGilligan's biography mentions the episode early in the war when Hitchcock "supervised the re-editing and dubbing" of two MoI propaganda films, in order to make them more acceptable to American audiences: *Men of the Lightship* (produced for the MoI in 1940) and *Target for Tonight* (1941).[3] He does not give details; the standard DVD release version of each film is the British original; nobody seems yet to have investigated the actual work that Hitchcock did on them. But his re-worked versions do survive.[4]

The changes to *Target for Tonight* are relatively minor, but the changes to *Men of the Lightship* are much more radical: it acquired a new title, *Men of Lightship "61,"* and its running-time was cut down by one-third, from 24 minutes to 16. Hitchcock clearly devoted serious time and care to this reworking, and the episode constitutes, at the very least, a significant footnote to the complicated story of his move from Britain to Hollywood and the tensions surrounding it.[5] He had come under attack at the time for staying in neutral America while Britain was at war, and this urgent re-editing work for the MoI was one of several ways in which he in effect, though in this case unobtrusively, answered those critics.

Enlisting Hitchcock

A crucial aim of the Ministry's Films Division, from the start of the war in Europe in September 1939, had been to get its output widely shown in still-neutral America, in order to increase public sympathy for the British cause. This needed careful calculation, if it was to overcome two major obstacles: political resistance to anti-isolationist propaganda and resistance on the part of the popular audience to British cinema. Early short films such as *London Can Take It* (1940), stitched together from vivid actuality footage of the effects of the aerial Blitz of late 1940, made an impact in America, but the Ministry was also by then financing more ambitious longer films of a drama-documentary type, pre-eminent among them being *Men of the Lightship* and *Target for Tonight*. These dramatize respectively an actual event, the destruction in January 1940 of a North Sea lightship by Nazi bombing, and a "typical" one: a late-1940 RAF bombing raid over Germany, undertaken as if in revenge for that kind of outrage. In the course of their narratives, the films celebrate the understated heroism of the crews of lightship and aircraft. With a single exception, the cast are servicemen enacting their real-life roles.

Both films had immediate success with British critics and audiences. A report of March 1943 showed that they had become the two most profitable of all government-sponsored releases up to that point.[6] A review in August 1940 in the political weekly the *New Statesman* testified that "the effect of

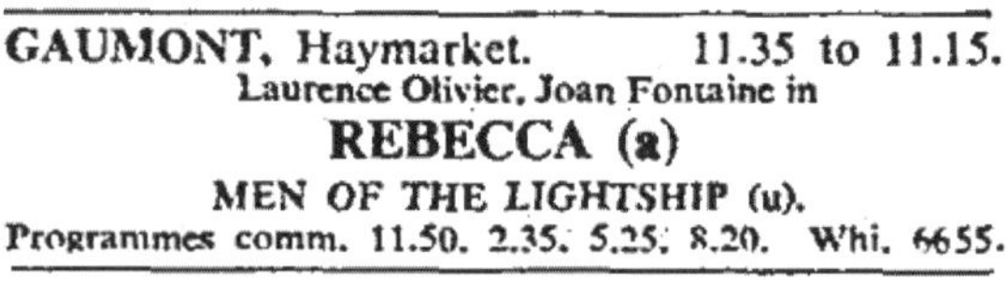

GAUMONT, Haymarket.   11.35 to 11.15.
Laurence Olivier, Joan Fontaine in
REBECCA (a)
MEN OF THE LIGHTSHIP (u).
Programmes comm. 11.50. 2.35. 5.25. 8.20. Whi. 6655.

Figure 1. Advertisement in the Entertainment columns of *The Times*, 29 July 1940.

Men of the Lightship on an ordinary audience enjoying an average programme was electric."[7] The reviewer may well, in fact, have seen the film in the same program as Hitchcock's own first Hollywood production, *Rebecca* (1940), on its initial run in the West End of London, since that was one of the several high-profile supporting slots negotiated by the Ministry (see fig. 1).

Despite the spectacular impact made by *Men of the Lightship* in Britain, Bernstein was quickly deflated by finding that the companies he invited to distribute the film in America, RKO and Fox, were reluctant to do so, "chiefly because the commentary and voices were unsuitable for those markets."[8] There was also a feeling that its pace was too slow. This was certainly the view of John Grierson, founding father of the British documentary movement, who was now running the new National Film Board of Canada and coordinating its own propaganda efforts. Looking back in February 1941 over the initial months of MoI production, he wrote to Bernstein from Ottawa that

> in general the films are slow, roundabout and far more concerned with sympathy than action. Sympathy you can take for granted. It is the direct activist style that will create confidence and participation . . . I don't like to call it dullness, but certainly there is a lack of narrative lift.[9]

He cited *Men of the Lightship* as an example of this slowness, and Bernstein, in forwarding the letter to colleagues, endorsed his comments. But by this time Hitchcock was at work on speeding up this particular film, and may already have finished the job.

After the refusal by RKO and Fox, Bernstein had taken rapid action. As he wrote later to a colleague in a lengthy summarizing memo, dated 3 April 1941:

> We therefore telegraphed Hitchcock and asked him if he would undertake re-editing and re-dubbing the voices. He agreed, and I discussed the suggestion with you, when it was arranged that I should cable Hitchcock and ask him the cost of this work. Hitchcock replied: "Will take care of all costs myself for the time being."[10]

As soon as Hitchcock's involvement became known, the MoI was attacked by his bitterest critic of the time, Michael Balcon, who had evidently offered, without success, to have the editing work done free of charge at his own base, Ealing Studios. He wrote to the Head of Films Division, Jack Beddington, that "It is particularly galling to people over here to have work of this nature tampered with by people so far removed from actualities . . . anti-Hitchcock feeling is very strong."[11]

But of course it made good sense for the re-editing to be done by someone who was much closer to the realities of the American market than Ealing was. Hitchcock was ideally positioned between the two countries and the two cultures, between American audiences and the aesthetics of British documentary production (his relationship to documentary is discussed in the final section of this article). A memo from Bernstein in late January 1941 suggests that he had by then made good progress:

> Alfred Hitchcock phoned me from Hollywood on Friday night (2 A.M. actually) to say that Hutchinson of Twentieth Century Fox Films had agreed to release Hitchcock's re-edited version of this film throughout the United States and Latin America, on a commercial basis.[12]

Figure 2. Early screening in Connecticut of
the re-edited version (March 1941).

It is clear, anyway, that by the start of April 1941 *Men of
Lightship "61"* had entered U.S. distribution, giving it a chance
to do its bit in encouraging pro-British sentiment—many
months before the Pearl Harbor attack of 7 December tipped
the U.S. into joining the war. Bernstein's memo of 3 April,
already quoted, summarized the position thus:

> The film has now been successfully cut and the
> voices re-dubbed, and Robert Sherwood has done
> the commentary . . . Cdr Jarratt saw the film in

America, and thinks it is excellent and that it will be
a great success.[13]

There is evidence of a screening in Connecticut as early as
March 1941, linked to the campaign to raise funds for "Allied
Relief": the word "Added" (to the scheduled program) in the
advertisement suggests a strong topical impetus (see fig. 2).
The film was certainly shown in Wisconsin in April, and in
Florida and Texas in May, and we can surely assume that
these fragmentary surviving records represent just "the tip of
an iceberg" of nationwide screenings.[14]

Men of the Lightship

The film "reconstructs" (the term used on the original
credits) the shocking bomb attack by German planes on a
lightship off the East Coast of England, early in 1940. This is
the basic narrative:

We are introduced to the crew of Lightship 61 and its
skipper as they anticipate a period of shore leave;
official arrangements are confirmed for a relief boat,
Argos, to take over.

From on board the lightship, a floating mine is
spotted, and a combined operation between crew
members and a passing naval ship succeeds in
blowing it up.

Later, two planes approach, but it is assumed
that, even if they are German, they will respect the
neutrality of a lightship, as in the war of 1914-1918.
But they dive-bomb the lightship repeatedly,
attacking with bombs and machine-gun fire. The
skipper is wounded, the lifeboat is lowered.
Meanwhile, the dispatch of the Argos has had to
be delayed.

The lifeboat is filled, the lightship sinks, the planes
depart, the men row away. Eventually the Argos
arrives at the location, but finds nothing.

By now the men are exhausted and cannot continue their heroic efforts. The boat and the bodies are washed up on the East coast.

The most immediately noticeable change in the U.S. version of the film, as re-edited by Hitchcock, is the provision of a different voice-over commentary at the start and the end. But the film itself has been quite radically reworked, in ways that are summarized in Chart 1 below. Hitchcock's strategy has been variously to *delete* whole scenes, to *compress* scenes, to *transpose* scenes; to *transpose* shots, and to *trim* shots; to *eliminate* voiceover commentary from the body of the film, and to *redub* some lines of dialogue. The overall effect is to reduce the running time, as already noted, from 24 minutes to 16, and to provide a more streamlined and linear narrative, one calculated to appeal more effectively to an American audience.

But it is essential to note, at the start, that this is emphatically not a case of a dull film being "saved," of a staid documentary being invigorated by commercial know-how. *Men of the Lightship* itself had brought together personnel from the commercial industry and documentary. Its producer, Alberto Cavalcanti, was about to move to Ealing Studios to work on features as well as documentaries for Hitchcock's own long-time associate Michael Balcon, while the main previous experience both of its director, David Macdonald, and of its writer, Hugh Gray, had been in 1930s feature production.[15] Moreover, Gray was an old and valued friend of Hitchcock's: they were classmates at school, and in the 1960s Hitchcock would personally finance him for a year of research and writing in Paris.[16] It is frustrating not to be able to find any evidence of communication between the two men over this particular film—Gray was by then serving in Europe, and time was short—but Hitchcock must surely at least have noted his name on the credits and respected the professionalism of the film's structure, centered on one familiar kind of belligerent threat, the floating mine, efficiently dealt with, followed by a second, the air attack, that could not have been foreseen or repulsed.

The script is also adroit, if predictable, in the way it sketches in something of the personalities of the crew members, alternating between their scenes and the action scenes, and between Lightship 61 itself and the wider operation of which it is part (involving scenes at the control center at Trinity House and on board the sister ship Argos). It is no surprise to find that the film was a major hit in Britain, nor that Bernstein and his MoI colleagues should have been so keen for American audiences to see it—to be outraged by the Nazi atrocity and impressed by the quiet heroism of its victims.

The complex job Hitchcock did in tightening up the film for American consumption does not mean that the original editing was loose—far from it. It was the work of one of the great professionals of documentary, Stewart McAllister, known above all for his collaborations with Humphrey Jennings; on *Listen to Britain* (1942) they even share a joint final credit, analogous to the celebrated joint Powell-Pressburger one, for "Direction and Editing." In 1983, most unusually for an editor, McAllister had a book devoted to him, written by Dai Vaughan—himself a working film editor as well as a distinguished critic and novelist—and including a full eight pages that analyze the subtleties of his work on *Men of the Lightship*.[17] Vaughan, who died in 2011, does not mention the existence of the Hitchcock re-edit, and may not have known about it.

Men of Lightship "61"

For ease of reference, Chart 1 divides the original film into numbered sections, juxtaposing its narrative with details of the Hitchcock re-edit.

As already noted, the immediate problem identified by American distributors, and at once addressed by Bernstein and Hitchcock, was a verbal one: the commentary and the accents. Hitchcock quickly gained approval for his suggestion that he should work with the playwright Robert Sherwood to supply a new Foreword and Afterword. In both versions, the Foreword (section 3) does a necessary job of concise factual

	Men of the Lightship Summary of action	Men of Lightship "61" Summary of changes
1	Newspaper headlines from early 1940: Nazi bombing of the East Dudgeon lightship	
2	Credit titles	Adjusted credits, cleaner type
3	Introductory images, with voice-over Foreword	Changed text and different voice
4	Conversation on deck: turn off fog signal, relief period coming soon	(adjustment to dialogue)
5	Below, getting up Establish characters, and their keen anticipation of relief. Lofty takes tea to the Skipper	Part retained; part cut; part compressed . . . and moved to later*
6	Voice-over orients us Trinity House: confirm plan for relief by another boat, Argos	No voice-over
7	Voice-over orients us Argos: making preparations for relief	No voice-over
7a		*moved from earlier: below deck: Lofty takes tea to the skipper
8	Lightship 61: crew climb mast, deal with the light mechanism	DELETED
9	Various other activities, work and relaxation: meanwhile we see a floating mine nearby	DELETED the anticipatory shots of the mine
10	Toss coin to decide who is to throw out slops: Lofty loses, wind blows contents of pail back in his face and then he sees the mine	DELETED all this until the sighting of the mine
11	Quick response to mine, crew sets out on lifeboat to deal with it, distress signal is fired	Some trimming of shots
12	A passing ship takes note and moves close; a squad of their men fire rifles to explode the mine, cheered by the men from 61	Re-cutting and tightening (to cover complex action quicker)
13	More singing and relaxation below deck, Lofty exits	Compressed
14	Couple on deck observe two planes approaching. Lofty joins them. No sense yet of danger	
15	The planes are German, and launch a fierce attack The skipper is wounded.	Minor transposition of shots
15a		Two more attacks are brought forward*
16	Trinity House: crisis elsewhere, so Argos is diverted – relief of 61 will be delayed.	
17	Argos: message received and acted on	
18	Five new attacks by German planes	*The three remaining attacks – with minor transposition of shots
19	Attacks continue: crew get into lifeboat, and are fired on there	
20	Images of the inside of the abandoned lightship	
21	Crew watch the lightship sink as the planes fly off	
22	Argos is baffled by not being able to find Lightship 61	DELETED
23	Crew keep rowing – days pass – getting weaker	
24	"Wish I was in the pub": we see and hear women, in the pub	DELETED all the pub material
25	Exhaustion – one man breaks down Land is sighted, but it's too late	
26	Boat washes up in the surf: final voice-over	Changed text and different voice

Chart 1

Opening Commentary

Men of the Lightship	*Men of Lightship "61"*
Year in, year out, all round our coasts, the beam of the lightship shines through the night, and its siren pierces the fogbanks.	To men who sail the seven seas, the lightship has always been a symbol of humanity – a symbol as sacred as the Red Cross.
Light and fog signals reach vessels of all nations equally, and for three centuries lightships and lighthouses were considered international.	The lightship has done its job in peace or war – giving warning of danger to sailors of all nations. It has been a guiding beacon for friend and foe alike.
300 years of warfare left them untouched, from the day when Louis the XIVth told his navy, "I am at war with England, but not with humanity."	Night and day for hundreds of years, off the perilous coast of England, the East Dudgeon lightship has ridden the foggy, stormy waters of the North Sea, sending its friendly signals to ships and men. During the first world war of 1914 to 1918 never once was this exposed, undefended lightship threatened by enemy action. But 1940 has brought into the North Sea a new kind of war – a new kind of enemy.
From that day, until the 29th of January 1940 . . .	

Chart 2

and dramatic orientation. Comparing the two, one sees how the text has been made simpler and less insular for a non-British audience (chart 2).

The insular "our coasts" become "the seven seas." Three centuries, 300 years, Louis XIV, the specific January date: these historical details are replaced by a single, instantly graspable reference point, the 1914-18 war, and the universal symbol of the Red Cross. Meanwhile the North Sea (twice), East Dudgeon, and the date of 1940 are set up as pragmatic coordinates for the action that follows.

Neither version identifies the speaking voice, either on the credits or in publicity, but a GPO Film Unit memo of 13 July 1940 authorized a payment of £5 for this commentary work to the actor Robert Newton, who had recently played the romantic lead in Hitchcock's last film before leaving for America, *Jamaica Inn* (1939).[18] Once one has this piece of archival evidence, the voice on *Men of the Lightship* does indeed become recognizable as his. The accent is lucid and unpompous, and does not in itself seem to require changing, but Hitchcock obviously needed someone close at hand to speak the new lines by Sherwood. He initially planned to use Robert Montgomery, and may have done so, though the voice on the re-edit is not as distinctive as Newton's is on the original.[19]

The other half of the Sherwood commentary (section 26) will be considered in its chronological place at the end of this section. Meanwhile, Hitchcock addressed the issue of dialogue. It is sometimes said that—as implied in the Bernstein memo quoted above—he did a wholesale "re-dubbing" both of this film and of *Target for Tonight*, but if he considered the idea he must have rejected it very quickly. For better or worse, these are modest, often self-deprecating, Englishmen: imposing American voices on them, or even Hollywood-English voices via actors like Ronald Colman or Nigel Bruce, would be anomalous. Instead, Hitchcock eliminates some of the dialogue altogether, and unobtrusively re-dubs certain lines to amend the words rather than the accents.

This process begins at once, in scene 4, the establishing scene on deck. The two men are waiting to go on leave, but are worried that the fog may come back and prevent the relief ship taking over. The older says to the younger: "Might come back for a week, and you getting married next Tuesday and all." The re-dub makes it less oblique: "Might come back for a week, and mess up your wedding next Tuesday."

The change is made easier by the fact that the words are spoken, in both versions, against an image of the sea. This part of the original film's dialogue had itself been separately recorded: an informative 1944 article in a British journal notes that "Dialogue was post-synchronised for the exteriors; quality is good but synchronism variable."[20]

Figure 3. Hitchcock's redubbing is made easy by the fact that the speaker (left) faces away from the camera.

In other exterior scenes, Hitchcock makes similar small adjustments, again in the interests of clarity. In scene 17, for instance, the sister ship, Argos, gets a message to postpone its scheduled relief of Lightship 61—which is now, as we know but the Trinity House depot does not, under attack from Nazi planes—in order to deal with a crisis elsewhere. The radio operator who takes the message reports to his captain: "Spot of bother from the depot, sir." The redub simplifies this: "Here's word from the depot, sir."

But in one scene (the start of section 12) Hitchcock subtly adjusts the dialogue's content. Spotting a floating mine, the lightship crew fire a distress signal. Cut to the other boat, which is within sight and earshot. One officer asks "What was that?" and gets the reply "Sounded to me like another ruddy mine, sir." The line is neat: "another" mine emphasizes that these are dangerous waters, and there is irony in the fact that this detonation is not in fact a mine but a call to help dispose of one. But Hitchcock's redub—aided again by the fact that the speaker is facing away from the camera (fig. 3)—flattens this out, preferring to go straight to the point: "What was that?" "Sounded like a distress signal."

Figure 4

This process of simplification is Hitchcock's basic strategy, not only on the verbal level but, more radically, in the editing, in both macro and micro terms—adjustments to the overall narrative and, often, to the shot-by-shot construction. Nowhere is this more striking than in the episode (section 10) of the floating mine itself, whose sighting triggers the distress signal. In the original, we see the mine, in two ominous cutaway shots, before it is spotted by any of the crew (fig. 4). It is a small but effective instance of editing for suspense, as so often expounded and practiced by Hitchcock himself (the bomb under the table, which we see but the characters don't). In his book on McAllister, Dai Vaughan makes much of the very precise editing of the sequence, not simply the cross-cutting itself ("to create anticipatory tension by intercutting is a familiar enough device") but a further range of associations created around the cuts.[21] Hitchcock again flattens out the complexities, and there is an obvious irony in the way he thus eliminates the most "Hitchcockian" element in the whole of the original film, the moment of anticipatory tension. Instead, we see the mine for the first time when it is spotted from the rail of the ship by Lofty, the crew member who has been most strongly established as a distinct character (figs. 5 and 6).

Figure 5

Figure 6

Whether or not he was aware of it, Hitchcock was thus reverting to the terms of the script written by his old friend Hugh Gray.[22] But in the lead-up to this key moment (scenes 5 to 10), he has made big changes to Gray's structure, as the chart indicates. This re-edit has two connected functions: to lead

Figure 7. An iconic British teacup moment which Hitchcock takes care to preserve.

more quickly to the action, and to shorten drastically the affectionate presentation of the crew members and of the very English understated humor of their dialogue. Even if wholesale redubbing was not a realistic option, this humorous dialogue could at least be cut back.

The main focus of the humor is Lofty—named thus, of course, because he is short in stature, just as his pet tortoise is named Lightning. Originally, the crew were played by professional actors; producer Cavalcanti found the results "totally unconvincing," and on his orders they were replaced by authentic seamen, with the one exception of Lofty, played by Leonard Sharp, an experienced character actor.[23] Sharp fits in perfectly well, and Hitchcock respects and retains his role in taking tea to the Skipper (fig. 7) and, soon after, spotting the floating mine. But he cuts out the comedy that leads up to that (his misjudgment of the wind direction, so that the slops get blown back in his face), and he not only shortens the below-deck business but breaks it up into two parts. We thus get a quick sketch of the crew and of their humanity (starting in scene 4 with the reference to the imminent wedding) and their humor, but without the danger, for an American audience, of their outstaying their welcome.

Comparison between the two films at this point underlines the sheer care and detail of Hitchcock's work on the re-edit. The lengthy section 5 in the original ends with a sequence of 15 shots; Lofty prepares to take tea to the Skipper, then finds his way through the ship, and delivers it. Hitchcock (a) postpones this, until after the contextual scenes at Trinity House and on board the Argos, and (b) shortens it, using only shots 1-2-3-4-8-15. The postponement compensates, as it were, for the loss of the build-up to the mine-spotting, so that this doesn't come too abruptly, while the shortening simply accelerates the momentum: the original has 15 shots in 78 seconds, and the re-edit, without any breach of smooth continuity, has 6 shots in 42 seconds. Lofty leaves with the tea, then brings it to the Skipper, omitting all of the strictly dispensable shots en route.

Two subsequent scenes, the two main action scenes of the film, demonstrate similar care in the re-editing. Section 12 involves elaborate co-ordinated maneuvers between the lifeboat in which crew members set out to pull the mine away from the lightship, and the naval ship which then obliges them by detonating it harmlessly with a rifle barrage. Here, Hitchcock streamlines the action not so much by deleting shots as by shortening them. His version has 24 shots, against 27 in the original, but the running time is cut by more than half: from 2 minutes 16 seconds (Average Shot Length 5 seconds) to 1 minute 5 seconds (ASL 2.7 seconds). There is no radical change here, simply a skillful speeding up, without the sacrifice of any lucidity in the presentation of a complex piece of teamwork.

The threat averted is followed by one that is unresistible, forming the central action, and indeed the *raison d'être*, of the film: sections 15-18-19, the air attack on the defenseless lightship. There is no temptation here to speed up the cutting rate: the original is powerfully shot and edited, based on vivid alternation between the viewpoints of attackers and of victims—a fluency made possible by the cooperation of the British Air Ministry, who were happy, once they had been convinced of the film's potential propaganda value, to put a variety of planes and pilots at the Unit's disposal.[24] The planes attack repeatedly; we cut away to the Trinity House controller who is frustratingly, at this moment, postponing the dispatch of the relief ship Argos, and then to the Argos itself as it receives the order; then back to the aerial bombardment that culminates in the survivors abandoning ship. Hitchcock's main alteration here is to "front-load" the action, giving us much more of the attack and its devastating effects *before* the cutaway to Trinity House and Argos. Once again this seems to make sense as a way of engaging the American audience, hitting them as hard as possible before risking the drop in tension.

Though the tempo of the attacks themselves is not changed, close analysis shows that Hitchcock, here as elsewhere, makes a number of small, unobtrusive, trims and transpositions. Anyone who has done archival research on the production of some of his later films will be familiar with "Mr. Hitchcock's Cutting Notes": documents that transcribe his reactions to seeing a provisional cut of a reel of film. Instructions range from the use of a different take, to the loss or insertion of a reaction shot, right down to the shaving even of two or three frames here and there. Documents of that kind survive from Hitchcock's fine-tuning, in 1944, of *Bon Voyage* and *Aventure Malgache*, and it seems likely that he operated in the same way in watching and re-watching *Men of the Lightship*. In section 11, the mechanics of firing the distress signal from the lightship are depicted in an awkwardly protracted shot of 10 seconds: the awkwardness is rather eloquent, showing the physical difficulty of the process and adding some tension, as we wait for ignition. Hitchcock prefers to cut out the waiting, making it a four-second shot: no sooner do we grasp what we are being shown than it fires. Both versions are effective in their different contexts, aimed at different audiences. Of his many small adjustments to the air attacks, one is especially neat. A crew member, one who has not been foregrounded in the scenes below deck, observes the planes going over, and, a few shots later, flinches back inside a doorway. Hitchcock cuts the second shot and reserves it for later, for use at another dramatic moment. Again, it is hardly

Figures 8, 9, 10, and 11. The skipper is shot: the image itself is riddled with bullets as he thinks of his wife. McAllister and Cavalcanti create a typically bold rapid montage, which Hitchcock respects and retains.

a necessary change, but one that demonstrates his drive to fine-tune the film as carefully as if it were one of his own.

After the attacks and the sinking of the ship, the lifeboat scenes (section 19 onward) are left virtually intact: they are given more concentration by the deletion of two scenes that take us elsewhere. The sister ship Argos provides a clear strand in the narrative of *Men of the Lightship*: it is ready to take over from Lightship 61 (section 7), it is diverted to other duties (section 17), and then it arrives at the location, baffled to find nothing there (section 22). Hitchcock sacrifices this third appearance, just as he eliminates the human touch of the cutaway to loved ones at home. He keeps the line "Wish I was in the pub," but deletes the brief scene of the cheerful women drinking there. Like the third appearance of the Argos, this answers an earlier scene: when the skipper of the lightship was wounded by bullets from the Nazi plane (section 15), a rapid subjective montage (figs. 8, 9, 10, and 11) included a shot of the woman we now see in the pub, presumably his wife. But Hitchcock's strategy for the final scenes is to focus on the exhausted crew, allowing no distraction from them until the death of the last of the men when in sight of land.

He could easily have cut out the earlier view of the wife as well, along with the rapid montage of which it formed part, "a fusillade of little shots" affectionately analyzed by Dai Vaughan: it features also brief glimpses, likewise only a few frames each, of the Skipper's canary.[25] That montage, a *tour de force* by Stewart McAllister, is not in Hugh Gray's script, and it jars unashamedly with the more sober documentary mode of the rest of the film. Leaving it in could be seen as a mark of respect by Hitchcock to McAllister, to the team of which he was part, to British documentary, and to the wartime work which Bernstein and his colleagues were starting to do with such success.[26] If he had not approached the re-editing work with this basic respect for the original, he could hardly have done the job so effectively. By now we are close to the end, and the final voiceover commentary is much closer to the original here than it was at the start, as illustrated in Chart 3.

The re-wording is more expansive and more explicit, taking care to give a brief explanation of when and how the bodies were found: a minor early illustration, perhaps, of Hitchcock's sense of a distinction between British and American audiences, the latter liking to have points more clearly spelled out. The defiant first-person rhetoric of the final two sentences obviously had to be changed, but Sherwood still ends on a powerful note.

Hitchcock and Documentary

What, finally, can we take away from this hitherto obscure episode in Hitchcock's career? It provides further evidence, if any were needed, against the attacks on him that were launched at the time by Michael Balcon and others: far from being a "Deserter," the word used in the headline of Balcon's notorious article of May 1940, Hitchcock was, from an early stage, operating vigorously in Hollywood in the British interest, not

Closing Commentary

Men of the Lightship	Men of Lightship "61"
	Italics: commentary retained from original **Bold: new commentary**
On January the 31st, a new light vessel is towed out to the East Dudgeon station.	*On January the 31st, a new light vessel is towed out to the East Dudgeon station.*
[images of drifting and wreckage; no words]	**As dawn arose on the morning of February the 1st, there was still no news of the ill-fated lightship number 61 or its crew. It was not until several days later that a resident of an east coast resort brought in the news that . . .**
The men of the East Dudgeon Light died of cold and hunger and wounds on the sands of the East coast.	*The men of the East Dudgeon* **Lightship Number 61** *died of cold, hunger and wounds on the sands of* **England's** *East coast.*
Their story is only one episode in a war of unparalleled horror.	**This** *story is only one episode in a war of unparalleled horror.*
The Nazis must be stopped. We must – we can – we *will* – stop them.	**Many men go down to the sea in ships, but surely no men ever died a braver death than these defenceless heroes of Britain's Lightship service.**

Chart 3

only through the high-profile anti-isolationist feature film *Foreign Correspondent* (1940) but also, soon after, through this unobtrusive and uncredited, but committed and craftsmanlike, work for the MoI. But the battle over Hitchcock's patriotism was won a long time ago.[27] He and Balcon would eventually resume their warm friendship. Of greater interest, now, is the incentive which the episode gives to rethink Hitchcock's relationship to the British documentary movement.

It is tempting to place the two in simple opposition. Talking to him about *The Wrong Man* (1956), Truffaut argued that "your style, which has found its perfection in the fiction area, happens to be in total conflict with the aesthetics of the documentary."[28] Writing in 1930, John Grierson had famously characterized Hitchcock's early films as "unimportant," urging him to "give us a film of the Potteries or Manchester or Middlesborough [three industrial areas], with the personals in their proper place and the life of a community instead of a benighted lady at stake."[29] Hitchcock declined the invitation, and followed his own path, as did Grierson himself, then at the start of a successful decade promoting government-sponsored documentary film in Britain and beyond.

And yet the two paths, and the two conceptions of cinema, can be seen as complementary and overlapping, as much as oppositional. In that same article, Grierson called Hitchcock "the sharpest observer and the finest master of detail in all England," a view endorsed in 1949, on the basis of Hitchcock's 1930s films, by another critic with documentary affiliations, Lindsay Anderson, who praised "the authenticity of the `everyday locales' and the `authentic minor characters, maids, policemen, shopkeepers, and commercial travellers' populating the films. That is the summary given in *Alfred Hitchcock and the British Cinema* by Tom Ryall, who continues thus:

> We have already drawn attention to the semi-documentary opening sequences of *The Lodger*, *The Ring*, *The Manxman* and *Blackmail*, but many of the later thrillers also contain social vignettes and cameos which impressed critics with a disposition towards "documentary modes."[30]

Writing in between Anderson and Ryall, in 1974, Raymond Durgnat had argued that the opening sequence of *Blackmail*, in which the police go to collect a suspect, corresponds in every way to the canons of "semi-fictional" or "reconstructed" documentary which the thriving school of pre-Grierson documentary makers had used from the war years on and which the Grierson school was to adopt for such films as *North Sea* [1938, GPO Film Unit] and *San Demetrio London* [1943, Ealing Studios] (with, as usual, no acknowledgment that the commercial cinema had been there ten years before).[31]

Durgnat's reference here to "the war years" of 1914-18 is salutary in reminding us that documentary, both as a word and as a mode of filmmaking, long predates Grierson's alleged invention of the term in 1927. As near-contemporaries, born in 1898 and 1899 respectively, Grierson and Hitchcock were both formed in the British film culture of the interwar years, and drew, in their different ways, upon overseas influences from Hollywood and beyond in order to shape a fresh and distinctive path for the native product. Both were involved with the Film Society, established in London in 1925, and both were particularly struck by the impact, at the end of the decade, of the new Soviet films and theories: Grierson adapted Eisenstein's *Potemkin* for its Film Society screening in a double bill with his own film *Drifters* (1929), while Hitchcock ever afterwards acknowledged the inspiration of Kuleshov and Pudovkin.

It is a radical misreading of Grierson to regard his conception of documentary as a prosaically factual one. The foundational text in which he first uses the term is a 1926 review of Flaherty's *Moana*, celebrating aspects of it that have a more than purely "documentary value."[32] Paradoxically, documentary film would be defined by him (and by colleagues) as a mode that transcends the merely "documentary." Like others, he would try to find alternative labels to replace that word, but without success: as he wrote in the opening sentence of a manifesto in 1932, "Documentary is a clumsy title, but let it stand."[33] Cavalcanti too recalled his dislike of the word: "I thought that 'documentary' was

Figure 12   Figure 13

something that smells of dust and boredom."[34] Both men were constantly straining to make documentary more vivid and dynamic. It was Grierson who, as quoted above, articulated the need to liven up films like *Men of the Lightship*: "It is the direct activist style that will create confidence and participation . . . I don't like to call it dullness, but certainly there is a lack of narrative lift." In stepping in to sharpen up the film by re-editing, Hitchcock was in effect carrying out Grierson's own prescription—working with a third key contemporary from the film culture of the 1920s and the Film Society, Sidney Bernstein, who himself spanned the fields of feature film and documentary.[35]

A fascinating item linking Hitchcock with Griersonian documentary recently resurfaced after being forgotten for four decades: a 30-minute program, *Hitchcock on Grierson*, broadcast by Scottish Television in 1969 (fig. 12). The title is slightly misleading, in that Hitchcock was reading to camera (fig. 13), on the set in Hollywood of his current film *Topaz*, a commentary script written independently for him in Scotland: he did not supply new words of his own, any more than he devised new shots to insert into the Lightship film.[36] But it is significant that he had agreed unconditionally, without any negotiation, to front this Grierson tribute, and that he did some editing of the script when it arrived, making a number of judicious cuts of lines he was not happy with, mostly ones that referred to his own career.[37] Page one of the script asked him to say "But this is a film not about me— those paeans of praise must await another evening—but about John Grierson." Hitchcock simply cut out the eight words in the middle, between the dashes, and a few other passages like them.

Not long before, in 1967, in response to another transatlantic request, he had agreed to write a foreword to a reissue of the novel on which *The Lady Vanishes* was based, and had asked as usual for a complete draft to be written for him; the result was a long and digressive piece about the book's author, Ethel Lina White, written by her nephew. Understandably, Hitchcock decided against signing this, and instead supplied a much shorter piece based on quotes from the Truffaut interview.[38] This bears out the approach taken by Sidney Gottlieb in the introduction to his collection, *Hitchcock on Hitchcock*. He argues that even when others wrote articles for him (or scripts, as in the case of his lead-ins to the TV series that were written for him by James Allardice):

> It is safe to assume that Hitchcock in one way or another guided, supervised, reviewed, and/or approved the final copy before it went to press. What may or may not have been his own exact words originally became authorized (by him and then by his readers) as his words.[39]

If the words did not feel right, as in the case of the item on Ethel Lina White, he declined to authorize them; conversely, we can take his words about Grierson as a sincerely authorized tribute. Grierson is, just as much as he is himself, a "man of cinema"—the program's final celebratory words, spoken emphatically by Hitchcock to camera. The two men have started from a common perception:

> In the early days of the cinema, men like John began to learn that the motion picture camera didn't merely have to reproduce on celluloid anything placed horizontally before it. If it was placed in certain ways, with cunning artifice, it could convey emotional

aspects of whatever it was filming. Others had made the elementary discovery that it could tell stories, but John found it could observe and comment on a changing world.

I myself utilised this as one of the story tellers. Others, led by John, banded together to create social documents on film.

After telling the story of the way in which government sponsorship enabled the development of an alternate system, parallel to the one within which he had built his own career, he names names: "John now gathered around him a group of brilliant young men: Robert Flaherty, Cavalcanti, Basil Wright, Paul Rotha, Humphrey Jennings, Harry Watt."

Cavalcanti was producer of *Men of the Lightship*, Harry Watt was director of *Target for Tonight*. Both were in the process of moving into feature films at Ealing, using professional actors to tell topical stories. Cavalcanti and Jennings had worked together not long before, on the documentary *Spring Offensive* (1940), using another script by Hitchcock's friend Hugh Gray. Harry Watt had already worked with Hitchcock, credited for the marine "Special Effects" on *Jamaica Inn* (1939); looking back, he would describe Hitchcock as "the only British feature director we respected."[40] The boundary between documentary and fiction was a fluid and shifting one, in terms both of personnel and of method.

There was nothing anomalous, then, about Hitchcock being asked to cooperate on adapting the two MoI films for their American release. *Men of the Lightship*, the earlier and shorter of the two, was clearly the one that needed more work; as we have seen, far from imposing any kind of "Hitchcockian" framework on a drama-documentary original, he took it if anything in the reverse direction. No feature director in Britain or America could have been a more appropriate choice, more in sympathy with what the film was doing and how—and the results bear this out.

Notes

This essay is adapted from a chapter in *Hitchcock: Lost and Found*, authored jointly with Alain Kerzoncuf, for publication by the University of Kentucky Press in 2014. I am grateful to the Leverhulme Foundation for the award of an Emeritus Fellowship which made possible a visit to libraries and archives in the U.S. in late 2012. Many thanks also to Barbara Hall and colleagues at the Margaret Herrick library in Los Angeles; Rosemary Hanes and colleagues at the Library of Congress in Washington, D.C.; Karl Magee, university archivist at Stirling; Christopher Philippo; and Alain Kerzoncuf.

Abbreviations

AMPAS Academy of Motion Picture Arts and Sciences,
       Los Angeles, California
NA   National Archives, London
INF   Ministry of Information files, held at the NA
IWM   Imperial War Museum, London
SLB   Sidney L. Bernstein papers, held at the IWM

1. *Bon Voyage* (26 minutes) and *Aventure Malgache* (32 minutes) were shot by Hitchcock at Welwyn Studios, near London, early in 1944; the former was given a very limited release in Europe later in the year. After being out of circulation for decades, both are now available together on DVD, in a variety of editions.

2. Bernstein's official role was as one of two "Honorary Advisers" from the industry, reporting directly to the Director of Films Division, a post held for most of the war by Jack Beddington. It is clear that Bernstein worked as hard in his own post as if it had been a full-time salaried one; he visited the U.S. more than once, spending time with the Hitchcocks, among many other industry figures.

3. Patrick McGilligan, *Alfred Hitchcock: A Life in Darkness and Light* (Chichester: Wiley, 2003), 280-81.

4. The standard version of *Target for Tonight* is the Imperial War Museum's DVD from 2007; that of *Men of the Lightship* is available as part of volume 3 of the BFI's collection of GPO Unit Productions, *If War Should Come*. The Hitchcock re-edit of *Men of the Lightship* was viewed in a 16mm print at the Library of Congress in Washington in

November 2012. It is now possible to find the different versions on YouTube.

5. See Charles Barr, "Deserter or Honored Exile?: Views of Hitchcock from Wartime Britain," *Hitchcock Annual 13* (2004-05), 1-24, reprinted in Sidney Gottlieb and Richard Allen, eds., *The* Hitchcock Annual *Anthology: Selected Essays from Volumes 10-15* (London: Wallflower, 2009), 82-96.

6. NA: INF 1/58.

7. *New Statesman*, 3 August 1940. The brief review is not signed, but is likely to be the work of the magazine's regular film critic, William Whitebait (pseudonym of the playwright and critic G.W. Stonier).

8. Bernstein to E.St.J. Bamford, 3 April 1941. Bamford was an MoI administrator, not himself a member of Films Division. IWM/SLB, Box 3.

9. Grierson to Bernstein, 11 February 1941, circulated by Bernstein to colleagues the following day. IWM/SLB, Box 3.

10. Bernstein to Bamford, 3 April 1941. Despite McGilligan's claim that "there is no evidence he was ever reimbursed" (*Alfred Hitchcock*, 281), this same summarizing memo of 3 April shows that, although Hitchcock took no fee, his costs of $4428.10 were quickly repaid to him in full.

11. Balcon to Beddington, 20 November 1940. IWM/SLB, Box 2.

12. Bernstein to Bamford, 27 January 1941. IWM/SLB, Box 2..

13. Bernstein to Bamford, 3 April 1941. Arthur Jarratt was a Naval Officer who did varied wartime liaison work in the U.S. Like Bernstein, he had extensive experience in film exhibition.

14. See *Manitowoc Herald Times*, 21 April 1941; *Miami Daily News*, 27 May 1941; *Alto Herald*, 28 May 1941.

15. Cavalcanti, a Brazilian, already had considerable experience in French cinema as writer, art director, and avant-garde director, before joining Grierson's GPO Unit in 1933; he was based at Ealing from 1940 to 1946. David Macdonald spent all of his career in the commercial industry, apart from a short wartime spell in documentary, first as director of *Men of the Lightship* and then with the Army Film Unit, notably as producer of *Desert Victory* (1943). Hugh Gray's script credits included Alexander Korda's imperial epic *The Drum* (1938).

16. Gray (1900-1981) is now best known as the translator of two volumes of essays by the French critic André Bazin, *What is Cinema?* (Berkeley and Los Angeles: University of California Press, 1967 and

1971). He was an early Film Professor at UCLA, closely associated with the magazine *Film Quarterly*; see "Hugh Gray: In Memoriam," in *Film Quarterly* (spring 1981), 1. Hitchcock's correspondence with, and about, Gray, and the funding of his research in the 1960s, is found in the Hitchcock collection at AMPAS, 112.f-1337.

17. Dai Vaughan, *Portrait of an Invisible Man: The Working Life of Stewart McAllister, Film Editor* (London: British Film Institute, 1983), 46-53.

18. NA: INF 5/66.

19. "THINK SHERWOOD MONTGOMERY VERY GOOD" [i.e., very good choices]: part of an encouraging telegram from Bernstein to Hitchcock, 24 October 1940. IWM/SLB, Box 3. Unlike Robert Sherwood, Robert Montgomery is not mentioned again in these records, and the idea of using him may have been shelved.

20. H.A.V. Bulleid, "Famous Library Films no. 23, *Men of the Lightship*," *Amateur Cine World*, September-November 1944, 118-21, at 119. The fact of post-synchronizing is confirmed in Ministry documents found in NA: INF 5/68.

21. Vaughan, *Portrait of an Invisible Man*, 48-50.

22. Vaughan, *Portrait of an Invisible Man*, 49.

23. Cavalcanti's insistence, after seeing the initial rushes, on replacing most of the actors by non-professionals, is reported in Bulleid, "Famous Library Films no. 23, *Men of the Lightship*," 118, and Vaughan, *Portrait of an Invisible Man*, 46. The text of his forceful telegram of 1 March 1940 is found in NA: INF 5/66. Leonard Sharp's busy film career lasted from 1935 to 1958; he is probably now best remembered as the pavement artist in the final scene of the 1955 Ealing comedy *The Ladykillers*.

24. The Air Ministry's offer to supply resources is given in a letter of 28 March 1940, following earlier disagreements. RAF representatives had been arguing that the film ought to show aircraft flying to the defense of the lightship and chasing off the attackers, an argument so clearly foolish that they soon came round and agreed "to arrange forthwith facilities for the proposed lightship film in the form in which it is summarized in Mr. Hugh Gray's general treatment." The episode is covered more fully in Vaughan, *Portrait of an Invisible Man*, 47-48. Hugh Gray had done the treatment, based on a range of visits and consultations. Dialogue is credited to David Evans, who was present for much of the shooting. For all this, see NA: INF 5/66.

25. See Vaughan, *Portrait of an Invisible Man*, 50, for a shot-by-shot analysis.

26. Whereas Dai Vaughan credits this bravura passage to the film's editor, linking it to other instances of his work, Ian Aitken prefers to credit it to the film's producer, linking it to his notable record of experimentation in France and then England. See Aitken, *Alberto Cavalcanti: Realism, Surrealism and National Cinemas* (Trowbridge: Flicks Books, 2000), 65-67. Both authors, however, stress the sympathy between producer and editor: whichever of them took the initiative here, the other must have approved.

27. For a full discussion of the controversy over Hitchcock's wartime activities, see Barr, "Deserter or Honored Exile?"

28. François Truffaut, *Hitchcock*, revised edition (New York: Simon and Schuster, 1985), 240.

29. John Grierson, review in *The Clarion*, October 1930; reprinted in Forsyth Hardy, ed., *Grierson on the Movies* (London: Faber and Faber, 1981), 110.

30. Tom Ryall, *Alfred Hitchcock and the British Cinema* (Chicago: University of Illinois Press, 1986), 177. The Lindsay Anderson quotation is taken from his article "Alfred Hitchcock," in *Sequence* no. 9 (1949), 118.

31. Raymond Durgnat, *The Strange Case of Alfred Hitchcock* (London: Faber and Faber, 1970), 97.

32. "Of course *Moana*, being a visual account of events in the daily life of a Polynesian youth, has documentary value. But that, I believe, is secondary." From Grierson's review of the film in the *New York Sun*, 8 February 1926, reprinted in Forsyth Hardy, ed., *Grierson on the Movies* (London: Faber and Faber, 1981), 23-25.

33. John Grierson, "First Principles of Documentary," reprinted in Forsyth Hardy, ed., *Grierson on Documentary* (London: Collins, 1946), 78-89. The first section was originally published in *Cinema Quarterly* (winter 1932).

34. Jim Hillier, Alan Lovell, and Sam Rohdie, "Interview with Alberto Cavalcanti," *Screen* 13, no. 2 (1972), 42.

35. Bernstein's major involvement with documentary came through his wartime work at the Ministry, and later at Granada Television through the launch of the powerful and influential weekly series *World in Action* (1963-1998).

36. The credits of "Hitchcock on Grierson" include "Commentary: Jack Gerson." Gerson (1928-2012) was a Scot with extensive experience as a writer for television. Soon after providing this script for Hitchcock, he wrote several episodes of the celebrated police series *Z Cars*, which ran on BBC TV between 1962 and 1978.

37. The six-page commentary script, as sent to Hitchcock, is held in the Library at Stirling University, home of the Grierson archive. Peggy Robertson's letter to Scottish Television, accepting the commission on Hitchcock's behalf, is dated 9 December 1968.

38. Negotiations in 1967-68 over Hitchcock's Introduction to the reissue of the novel *The Lady Vanishes* are found in the AMPAS Hitchcock papers, 119.f-1381.

39. Sidney Gottlieb, ed., *Hitchcock on Hitchcock* (London: Faber and Faber, 1995), xiv.

40. Harry Watt, *Don't Look at the Camera* (London: Paul Elek, 1974), 121.

Figure 1

JOHN BRUNS

Hitchcock's Newspaper:
A "Thing in the Crowd"

1

In an illustration by the well-known English caricaturist Philip William May, *Man Reading Newspaper in Crowd* (fig. 1), we see a corpulent gentleman, sporting a top hat and carrying under his arm an umbrella, holding in two hands a rather fat newspaper whose bulky sheets threaten to envelope a young boy.[1] Given its substantial dimensions, we can safely assume the gentleman's newspaper is not a penny daily. Easily twenty-four inches wide, the newspaper is very likely a respectable six-penny journal—not exactly the sort of newspaper one spreads open wide in a crowd, hence the look on the young boy's face, which seems to be of slight surprise at the gentleman's unmindfulness. What this comic scenario reminds us of is that the newspaper is the very emblem of the modern urban crowd. Sold in sidewalk newsstands, purchased by bus and railway passengers, and left discarded in the streets where it is picked up again, the newspaper is found wherever there are crowds. Further, the newspaper layout itself creates a kind of crowd effect: its stories are crammed into columns that stand shoulder to shoulder and give to the physically dislocated and radically separate events they depict the illusion of order, coherence, and simultaneity. As Philip Fisher puts it, "The front page of the newspaper is itself a crowd, a mass of individuals who remain strangers to one another."[2] Further, the shape of the newspaper is always changing. It can be folded, rolled up tightly, even ripped apart. And when the newspaper is opened fully in a crowd, its

Figure 2

presence is not only seen but felt as well. Consider not only May's illustration, but the opening scene of Alfred Hitchcock's *Rich and Strange* (1932) when, with umbrella under arm, Fred Hill (Henry Kendall) opens his newspaper on a crowded train, much to the visible irritation of his fellow passengers.

Or turn to the image above (fig. 2), from Hitchcock's *Foreign Correspondent* (1940), which bears comparison with May's illustration. In it we see a similarly rotund man, also reading a newspaper, making his way through the crowded city (whose streets will be teeming, moments later, with umbrellas). Of course, the two images are not without significant differences—the most notable of which is that this second man is unmistakably a man of the cinema: he is the director himself, making his customary cameo appearance. And it cannot pass unnoticed that his newspaper is making its own cameo (in a film that takes the newspaper as its subject) at the moment of a rather obvious process shot. The use of rear projection, however much a studio technique, is one of Hitchcock's better-known signature effects. Hitchcock does not appear in the projection itself but in front of it, just as he does for his cameo in *Stage Fright* (1950). However, there is another man reading a newspaper who does appear in the projection, thus creating an odd doubling effect. Further, this particular cameo calls to mind another: from *Lifeboat* (1944), in which Hitchcock can be seen on a sheet of newspaper, hawking the "obesity slayer" named Reduco.[3] There are two images of Hitchcock on this newspaper: the first image is as his former, fatter self; the second as a slimmer, sadder self. The cameo itself is a mini-story, told in pictures. In *Foreign Correspondent*, Hitchcock is not in a crowd himself, though one is projected behind him while he reads a newspaper. In *Lifeboat*, Hitchcock is not in the film itself, but is projected onto a newspaper.

A strange association is established: the crowd, the newspaper, and the cinema. It is an alliance forged as early as Hitchcock's first films, though we have yet to take full measure of its strength—its durability as a central trope in Hitchcock's work. In one of the only essays to make note of Hitchcock's use of newspapers, Ina Rae Hark focuses only on *Foreign Correspondent*, *Saboteur* (1942), and *Lifeboat*. As we shall see, however, the newspaper's presence is everywhere in Hitchcock, from *The Lodger* (1926) to *Frenzy* (1972). Thus, unlike other well-known objects in Hitchcock, such as the lighter in *Strangers on a Train* (1951), the newspaper is not limited to a single film.[4] Further, Hark deemphasizes the newspaper as such in order to stress what it is meant to invoke: the democratic freedom of the press and the threats posed to it by the rise of Fascism. Even as she maintains that the newspaper is a privileged object throughout Hitchcock's career, she sees its function within Hitchcock as habitually narrative: "a newspaper's displaying a front-page photo of a wrongly accused man is a recurring trope, both before, during, and after the war years. In this regard newspapers err by regarding the ever-bumbling legal authorities as competent."[5] Treating the newspaper as a "metonymy for the functioning of democratic governments" or assigning it a plot function, Hark largely neglects the close interaction, both perceptual and tactile, between the newspaper and its handlers.[6]

It is true that Hitchcock's newspaper is something (for us as well as the characters within the film) to read. What is interesting in Hitchcock's films is the way their plots keep appearing in newspaper headlines and columns, almost always in distorted form (we know better, or think we know better, based on what we're privileged to witness). Even more interesting, however, is that Hitchcock's newspaper gets considerable hands-on attention. It is treated as more than a shapeless receptacle of narrative information: it is reshaped and torn apart, scratched, rolled up, used as a disguise, as a shield, as a telescope. In other words, Hitchcock's newspaper is enigmatic; often when it does appear, it is not just as a newspaper but as something else as well. When, for instance, in *Psycho* (1960), Marion Crane buys a newspaper in a vending machine at California Charlie's used car dealership, the newspaper signifies nothing more than itself—a social product not at all out of place. Then the newspaper begins to change. By the time Marion arrives the Bates Motel, the newspaper is no longer just a newspaper; it has been altered, recontextualized. Marion wraps what is left of the stolen $40,000 inside the newspaper—the very place she looks to find news of her crime. The link between Marion and her newspaper becomes even stronger moments later when Norman wraps Marion's corpse in the shower curtain. Now evidence of Norman's crime, Marion herself must be wrapped up and hidden from view. Both she and her newspaper are placed in the trunk of her car and sent to the bottom of the swamp. Think, too, of the newspaper in *Shadow of a Doubt* (1943). Like the ring that is exchanged between Uncle Charlie and his niece (and previously between Bruce Matthewson and Thelma Schenley), the newspaper circulates. But unlike the ring, the newspaper is in a state of continuous variation. As it passes from Mr. Newton to Uncle Charlie, then to Charlie, it passes through changes: first, it is the dependable home newspaper, then it is ripped apart, then folded into a toy barn, and finally it resurfaces intact in the Santa Rosa public library.

What follows in this essay is an attempt to recall the Hitchcock newspaper, to keep it front and center and not allow it to "disappear into the messages it transmits."[7] We cannot know too much of this singularly unusual Hitchcock object, and it is the purpose of this essay to determine its many vocations, not just its most prominent ones. One might argue that one of the newspaper's vocations is to act as a front for none other than Hitchcock's camera, for its "murderous gaze" to use William Rothman's well-known phrase. Like Hitchcock's camera, the newspaper is a harbinger of violence and death.[8] We often spot the newspaper at murderous moments in Hitchcock's films. In *Rear Window* (1954), Jefferies uses a pair of binoculars to spy on Lars Thorwald, who is seen standing before his kitchen sink, wrapping a saw and a large knife in a newspaper. But as this example suggests, we can link the newspaper not only with murder, but technologies of surveillance and spectacle (not simply because he is spying on Thorwald, but also because Jefferies is a photojournalist). The newspaper is indeed murderous, but, again like Hitchcock's camera, it is also spying, scrutinizing, knowing, dissimulating, and dissembling. For this reason, we ought to consider the many ways the newspaper functions at critical moments in Hitchcock's films, to attend to its conspicuous visibility and, as importantly, its shape-shifting materiality.

2

If the newspaper seems as ubiquitous as the crowd in Hitchcock, it is because the newspaper is the very emblem of the crowd—a recurrent object with far-reaching significance.[9] The newspaper, of course, is only one of many busy "things" that tend to surge to the foreground in the Hitchcock landscape. But no object is quite so intimately linked to the crowd as the newspaper; further, there is something terrifying about the cinematic treatment of reality itself that is mirrored in their relation. Hitchcock's newspaper is the thing in the crowd, the (secret) agent that leads us. The first step into a critical navigation of the crowded Hitchcock landscape—a step I wager is rather easy for the Hitchcock scholar to make—is to assume that objects (lighters, keys, bottles of wine, glasses of

Figure 3

Figure 4

milk, windmills, wedding rings, and so on) function as nonhuman agents. The next step is to allow a *thing* in Hitchcock to express itself.[10] Nevertheless, it is just as important to define or describe an agent (human or nonhuman), or say what it represents, as it is to look at the trace it produces, and see what visible effects it has on other agents. As we follow the newspaper, we register views of the Hitchcock landscape rarely seen.

One of Hitchcock's most unusual crowd scenes in which a newspaper figures prominently occurs in *Marnie* (1964), at the Atlantic City Race Course, where Marnie (Tippi Hedren) unexpectedly encounters a man in the crowd, a stranger from

Figure 5

Figure 6

her past. The scene begins with a curious sequence of shots (fig. 3-6). The first is a medium close-up of the unidentified man. Behind him are spectators, fixed with a variety of ocular prosthetics: not just the usual ones, such as eyeglasses and sunglasses, but binoculars as well (I count at least four pairs in fig. 5). We don't know what the stranger, who stands front and center in the frame, is looking at, but he is most certainly *not* looking at the race. We think he is looking at Marnie, who has come to the racetrack with Mark Rutland (Sean Connery). However, in the reverse shot that follows, which we can only assume is the stranger's point of view, neither Marnie nor Mark can be seen in the crowd. We cut back to the stranger, to find him holding a most unusual ocular prosthetic: a tightly rolled up newspaper that he holds up to his right eye and looks through. The next shot, again his point of view, is through the newspaper, which forms a slightly misshaped iris through which we see Marnie seated at a table, watching the race.[11] Across from her is Mark, who is looking through a pair of binoculars. There are a number of striking things about this particular shot. First, Marnie is seen turning around, away from the track, glancing almost directly into the camera. What gets her attention is unclear, though one suspects she has the feeling of being watched—there is, after all, a small army of lookers behind her, and one half-wonders if the man from her past is not the only one not watching the race.

What is more striking is the telescopic effect the rolled-up newspaper produces. Marnie and Mark are seen much too close up, compared with our previous point of view shot. The newspaper doesn't appear to be hiding a telescope within it, so how is it possible that a newspaper could produce such a view? This is not as odd a question as it seems, for the power of the newspaper is frequently given ocular, even proto-cinematic, qualities. As early as 1838, Galpin and Sturtevant's penny daily, *The Age*, claimed that a small sheet of newspaper is like "a camera obscura, which gives you the objects that pass before it the smallest possible compass, and yet in full perfection."[12] Consider, too, Frederick Knight Hunt who, in 1850, writes: "the newspaper is a great mental camera, which throws a picture of the whole world upon a single sheet of paper."[13] What is striking about these metaphors—the newspaper as *camera obscura*, the newspaper as *mens mentis obscura*—is that in spite of their conceptual clarity, it is difficult to figure out exactly how these newspapers work in such a way. Hunt's metaphor is barely interpretable. Is the newspaper both camera and projector? This seems to be the image Hunt asks us to see. But the newspaper is also a single sheet of paper, upon which the picture it records and projects is printed. Like the Lumière's *cinématographe*, the newspaper is capable of undergoing multiple transfigurations: it is camera, printer, and projector all in one. And yet the newspaper is somehow more: though proto-cinematic, it has no technical properties, no moving parts—or, more precisely, its moving parts are found in a great mind, a collective brain. As Gerald Stanley Lee put it in 1913, the newspaper is both "mass machine" and "crowd thinker."[14] If Hunt's description of the newspaper wasn't baffling enough, consider Lee's newspaper: it is a moving picture produced by crowds.

Hence the most striking thing of all in this scene from *Marnie*: the newspaper the stranger holds is not just impossibly telescopic but thaumaturgic, as it seems to produce Marnie and Mark out of thin air. If we are to trust the first reverse shot (fig. 4), Marnie and Mark are not in the stranger's line of view. The image we view through the newspaper is the visual equivalent of a *non sequitor*: this view of Marnie and Mark does not follow. Yet we are all the more confident that the stranger does indeed see them, for he then approaches their table. All we see of him is his torso, in front of which he carries the rolled-up newspaper. Fingering the newspaper with his right hand, he asks, "Pardon me, but you're Peggy Nicholson, aren't you?" Marnie is visibly rattled, but it is not clear who rattles her more: the stranger, or the man of whom he then speaks, a Frank Abernathy ("You remember *Frank*," he croons). Marnie asks him to leave, and he responds, "Aw, come on now honey, you're trying to pull my leg, aren't you?" Why is the newspaper so prominent at the beginning of this exchange? Why do we not see the stranger's head? And why, more importantly, is he holding the newspaper like that, middle and ring finger in the hole, gratuitously to the point of stylization? It hardly matters that, in a subsequent shot, he switches fingers (to index and middle); the point is that he is fingering this newspaper while probing this Miss Nicholson person. Is the stranger a nosy reporter? Or is he a pervert who likes to hang out in crowds?

When Mark returns to the table, we expect him to put the matter to rest. Yet he only adds to the confusion: not simply about the identity of the stranger (who simply should be

dismissed as a pest), but of the woman as well. Marnie asks
the stranger to leave. It is at this moment that Mark interrupts
the awkward exchange:

> MARK: Now why should any young lady want to pull
> *your* leg?
> STRANGER: Oh, sorry. I thought I recognized this lady.

With these words, the stranger begins to gently stroke the
inside of the newspaper with his two fingers.

> MARK: [to Marnie] Did he recognize you?
> MARNIE: No.
> MARK: [to Stranger] You did not recognize her.
> STRANGER: I said I *thought* I recognized her. I said I'm
> sorry.

A curious line of questioning here: rather than assure the
stranger that the young lady is not pulling his leg, is pulling
no one's leg, is not a leg puller, Mark instead asks the stranger
why any young lady should want to pull the stranger's leg. It
seems Mark is suggesting that the stranger is an ugly little
man that no young lady would want to look at, much less
touch. Yet Mark is, in effect, also telling the stranger, "excuse
me, but the young lady is pulling *my* leg, not yours." Mark
then turns to ask Marnie, "Did he recognize you?" But why
does Mark not ask the more likely (or more appropriate)
question in a situation such as this: "Do you recognize him?"
It's as if Mark is determined to rid Marnie of the obnoxious
stranger without letting her off the hook. But if Mark's
question is misdirected, Marnie's response is practically self-
incriminating ("He thought he did, but he was mistaken"
would be the best defense). By responding "no," Marnie
leaves open the possibility that she is someone to be
recognized by a stranger. Mark's final remark to the stranger,
"You did not recognize her," hardly puts the matter to rest.
Quite the opposite: Mark has more or less implied the
following: "You *did* recognize her, but perhaps you had better

pretend you did not." Thus what the stranger's newspaper zeroes in on (literally, as it creates an iris effect in fig. 4) is Marnie. In doing so, the newspaper shows us the considerable danger Marnie is in by having so many identities. One danger, of course, is that by having multiple identities she has no identity at all. This danger becomes lethal if we consider a real possibility that having no identity means any man could have his way with her and suffer no consequences. It doesn't matter to the stranger that she does not answer to the name Peggy Nicholson. Indeed, this gives him all the more reason to keep probing, to keep fingering. It takes a final threat of violence from Mark to put the stranger away for good. In probing too deeply, the stranger presses his luck.

There is another newspaper in this film, one that is not only visually linked with the stranger's newspaper, but with the suggestive line of questioning that comes with it as well—and not just the stranger's line of questioning, but Mark's too. Earlier in the film, we see a different finger gently stroking the inside of a newspaper, and it is Marnie's. She is scanning the classified ads of the *Philadelphia Inquirer*, searching for a position as payroll clerk. In one column we see multiple female occupations stacked one upon the other: seamstresses, pantry workers, receptionists. Next to it is another column, this one full of ads for housekeepers. The newspaper lists a hundred empty positions, all of them waiting to be occupied. It is the woman with no identity who can fill them all, and this is exactly what raises the threat of violence that Marnie faces in a crowd of hurtful watchers—a threat made very clear on her newspaper's front page. We get a good look at it when Marnie emerges from Pennsylvania Station and walks toward the camera. She pauses, and we see the newspaper in her right hand in perfect balance with her purse, which she clutches under her left arm. As is the case with so many newspapers in Hitchcock's films, this one cannot pass unnoticed. Indeed, we are meant to read its headline: "Crash Kills 118." This headline predicts Marnie's own literal crash, when her beloved horse Forio trips over the wall and throws Marnie to the ground. But Marnie's newspaper is also linked to the stranger's, which is rolled into a magic telescope through which we probe the woman with multiple identities—though perhaps not as many as 118. Further, the stranger's newspaper links the stranger to Mark, whose baffling line of questioning can hardly be considered a gallant effort to ward off cruel and hurtful watchers. Mark may be humiliating the nosy pervert, but he is also exposing himself as a bit of a sleazy correspondent. Mark, too, probes into the mystery that is Marnie, and his probing is more persistent, and more cruel, than the stranger's. To be sure, if there is a hint of sexual violence in the stranger's own line of questioning, it is Mark who carries out the violence in full force.[15]

As strange as these scenes from *Marnie* seem, they are by no means the only scenes in Hitchcock in which the newspaper plays multiple roles in the modern, urban crowd—as a thing to be read, a thing both probed and probing. We may recall a similar scene in *Notorious* (1946), in which Devlin (Cary Grant) and Alicia (Ingrid Bergman), also at a race track, are spied by a jealous Alex Sebastian. From high above in the box seating area, he is looking through a pair of binoculars while his mother sits next to him pretending to read a newspaper. One might argue of course that Mrs. Sebastian *is* reading the newspaper, and that the newspaper is nothing more than what it appears to be. This is why we feel Alicia is at least partially safe as she speaks in confidence with Devlin: the two aren't being watched. But we later learn, when Alicia does, that they *are* being watched. This casts some doubt as to whether Mrs. Sebastian's newspaper, like Alex's binoculars, is being employed for the most obvious of means. In the movies we can almost always spot the spy: he's the one reading the newspaper. I have in mind *Topaz* (1969), in which spies read newspapers and also pretend to read newspapers as they spy. Think, too, of the scene in *North by Northwest*—one of Hitchcock's great crowd films—outside the cafeteria at Mount Rushmore National Monument. The Professor (Leo G. Carroll) is sitting and reading a newspaper while Roger Thornhill (Cary Grant) stands next to him, looking through binoculars at the crowded face of Mount

Rushmore. Of course, the Professor isn't really reading the newspaper.[16] He is using the paper to disguise the fact that he is carrying on a conversation with his newly enlisted spy.

3

Perhaps the most famous newspaper of all in Hitchcock is the Newton family home newspaper in *Shadow of a Doubt*. The question, when we consider this newspaper, becomes "what is the connection between a home newspaper and the city newspaper and, more generally, between the home and the urban crowd?" Indeed, no newspaper in Hitchcock undergoes more change, attains more significance, moves more deceptively and travels more distance, than the *Santa Rosa Republican*.

It is the combination of visibility and vulnerability, in tension with Hitchcock's complex and ambivalent understanding of crowds, that the newspaper in *Shadow of a Doubt* foregrounds. Uncle Charlie's great blunder is that he fails to appreciate the enigmatic power of the newspaper: he rips out an incriminating story from his brother-in-law's evening newspaper—a column about the Merry Widow murderer—in the mistaken belief that in doing so he finds cover. But reading the newspaper is not always a private, solitary activity, as it is for Joe Newton. It can also be, as it is for Ann, very public. Despite the Newton family rule that the newspaper belongs to Joe and to no one else ("You've got papa's paper," says Roger to Uncle Charlie, to which his sister Charlie adds, "You know that's father's newspaper"), a copy of each daily edition of the *Santa Rosa Republican* can be accessed from the archives of the library. Uncle Charlie's private act of concealment is pointless because the story is already in public view. The newspapers in *Shadow of a Doubt* remind us that Santa Rosa is not a closed-off little world, blissfully ignorant of and free from its larger neighbors' urban nightmares. As many critics have noted, Hitchcock's film exploits elements of *film noir*, a style we associate with films that take place in big cities (New York, San Francisco, Los

Angeles). Robin Wood, in his celebrated reading of this film insists that we attend to its thematic oppositions: "the 'innocence' of small town American life; the apparent opposition of that innocence to a corrupt, perverted, and dangerous 'under-world.' " And Wood goes further: like David Lynch's *Blue Velvet* (1988), Hitchcock's film reveals that "innocence" and the "under-world" "are in fact intimately interrelated and interdependent."[17] What I will show here is that the newspaper is the thing that links the small town with the under-world—or more precisely, with *its* under-world. When night falls, Santa Rosa gets perverted and corrupted. But it gets very crowded as well.

The first newspaper we see in the film is not, it so happens, the *Santa Rosa Republican*. We catch a glimpse of an unnamed newspaper early in the very first scene in the film. We can't tell what newspaper it is because we can't see enough of it—nor may we even hazard a guess since we don't know what city we are in. All we know is that we are in a dark and shabby room in a boarding house. It is likely we are in Philadelphia, the place Charlie remembers being her Uncle's last city of residence. Yet it is just as likely that her uncle has moved on. Indeed, we may never know where we are in this opening scene, or what newspaper Uncle Charlie has next to him on the bed stand. But we do know this: stacked upon that newspaper is a wad of cash—the money he has stolen from the Merry Widows he has murdered—a pile so so large that part of it has tumbled to the floor below. Also on the newspaper is a bottle of water, two glasses, an ashtray, an opened wallet, and a few of Uncle Charlie's personal effects— the very clues to the Merry Widow's identity which the newspaper seeks. We know Uncle Charlie is on the run, and now we begin to sense that it is just a matter of time before a story of the Merry Widow murderer breaks.

At first glance, the Newton family newspaper, the *Santa Rosa Republican*, seems unaware of the Merry Widow murders, occupied as it is with news of a pending war (the film takes place in 1941). In a perceptive essay that examines maternal desire and American domesticity as represented in both *Shadow of a Doubt* and Hitchcock's remake of *The Man Who Knew Too Much* (1956), Elsie B. Michie makes a good deal of the newspaper in the former film:

> On his first night in the Newton household, Uncle Charlie appropriates Joseph Newton's newspaper, ostensibly to make it a playhouse for Ann (a perfect image of Uncle Charlie's desire to turn the written word into an emblem of domesticity for the girl child). Charlie's ulterior motive in playing this game is, however, to destroy the section of the paper that contains an article referring to himself. It is this paper that, when she steals it back, becomes the means for Charlie to discover her uncle's secret.[18]

Later in the essay, Michie echoes Rothman's point that it is when Charlie reaches the public library and reads the missing headline that her knowledge and ours, of what the ring's inscription "To TS from BM" means, for the first time coincide: "We see the text of the newspaper article displayed on the screen, read the information contained within it, and understand the inscription of the ring at the same moment that Uncle Charlie does."[19] Michie is absolutely right, I think, that the true horror of the newspaper is not that it reveals Uncle Charlie's identity as the Merry Widow murderer, but that Charlie finds in its lines her own story: a bright, talented young woman (Thelma Schenley, the TS on the ring) desires to strike out on her own but must, inevitably, as it was with her mother, become a wife (as Emma says, in the film's most heartbreaking scene, "I got married and . . . you know how it goes, you sort of forget you're you . . . you're your husband's wife"). However, I do think that we begin to understand this story well before we read the incriminating headline. Our knowledge, I argue, coincides with Uncle Charlie's, when he finds himself in the evening newspaper.

True, we are unable to read the incriminating headline when Uncle Charlie first finds it, as this pivotal shot begins just as Uncle Charlie turns the page of the newspaper so that the headline faces him, not us. Had Hitchcock not cut on this precise action, we may have caught a glimpse of the headline.

Figure 7

Instead, we must wait until his niece Charlie finds it in the public library. Still, we register *something* when he turns over the newspaper. And although we cannot see what he reads, our eyes probe the page of the newspaper that is now visible to us, the page Uncle Charlie has just finished reading: the "Santa Rosa Social and Club News" (fig. 7). What we see is also something of an incriminating story: in the left column, there is a photograph of a young woman (of Charlie's age) in modern dress and a sporting hat. She is moving forward, it seems, with confidence. In the right column, there is a photograph of a couple, perhaps newly wed. The woman in this second photograph is turned in the opposite direction of the woman in the first and clings adoringly, almost helplessly, to a man in uniform. In this way, the newspaper presents in stark visual terms what Michie rightly calls Uncle Charlie's "Manichean splitting of the world" into independent women and "true wives."[20] The "Santa Rosa Social and Club News" displays for us both the reasons for Uncle Charlie's crimes and his potential victims.

The next morning, we see the newspaper again when Uncle Charlie is reading in bed. Once more, the page visible to us is the

Figure 8

"Santa Rosa Social and Club News." As his sister Emma enters with breakfast, Uncle Charlie sets the paper down next to him, with the "Santa Rosa Social and Club News" section lying face up. Why has Uncle Charlie returned—or rather, why has Hitchcock returned us—to this same section of the newspaper? Why hasn't Uncle Charlie disposed of the newspaper entirely? Is he wrong to think he's in the clear simply by removing a page or two? What follows in this bizarre scene may help us understand more fully what this section of the *Santa Rosa Republican* is telling us, and why it is essential that we "read" a Hitchcock newspaper more carefully. As Emma pampers her little brother, she tells him that while he was sleeping, "the newspaper called up for an interview" with Uncle Charlie—and not just Uncle Charlie, but the whole Newton family.

Uncle Charlie becomes visibly disturbed and asks Emma why the newspaper happened to pick this particular family. We cut to a full shot of Emma (fig. 8) as she says "I told them we aren't a typical family." To the right of Emma we see the photograph of Uncle Charlie's niece that hangs on her wall. It is a photograph that Uncle Charlie had inspected closely when he first checked into his niece's bedroom, in an unsettling shot in which we see his ghostly face reflected as if superimposed—on the photograph. In this earlier shot, what is clear is that Uncle Charlie has a kind of bemused disdain for his niece—at least as she is depicted in the photograph. She is the head of her high school class, and easily destined for if not greatness then certainly independence. It is a class of only five, which suggests that in Santa Rosa, there are few young women who get this far, or even make the choice to try. As Emma's words suggest, Charlie is not "typical." But she is real, and there is a growing number of her kind out there, more than to her uncle's liking ("Emmy, women are fools!" he says). We see the photograph several more times, and each time we do, Emma speaks of the whole Newton family being in the limelight. Indeed, Uncle Charlie's visit has caught the attention of not just the Women's Club, but the newspaper, which called the Newton home asking for an interview. Emma also says that a man named Graham has also rung the Newton household, and that he wishes to ask questions, take pictures, and report their findings to the American people. Uncle Charlie tries to persuade Emma to turn down the offer, but she assures her brother that it would be no intrusion at all for the survey man to take their pictures: "Oh, he doesn't want us to dress up or anything . . . he just wants us to act the way we always do." The problem for women, of course, is that there is a big difference between the way they want to dress, the way they want to act, and the way they *should*. As the photograph depicts Charlie, one of five young women, dressed for success, the shot in which the photograph appears in turn depicts Emma, dressed to pamper men.

For Charlie, there is only one way for a woman to dress and act, and he enforces this view with ruthless violence. With his buttery voice, it sounds like he's only teasingly scolding his sister, "Why expose the family to a couple of snoopers?" But as he says these words, he holds a knife up, points it at Emma, and says "You ought to have better sense." At that moment, Charlie enters the room, dressed in an apron like her mother. Indeed, as the camera moves right to reframe young Charlie so she stands between her uncle, to her right, and her

Figure 9

mother, to her left, we see a striking similarity between the two women. On the wall directly above Uncle Charlie we see another picture, this one a drawing of two women in Victorian-style clothes (fig. 9). The older of the two is seated, tending to the dress of the younger woman, who stands next to her. The satisfied look on Uncle Charlie's face tells us that there is something reassuring in this picture of traditional femininity, and he is reassured all the more by the picture in front of him, of his doting sister and niece. What complicates the idea that Charlie's story may end up being her mother's after all is that other picture hanging on the wall, the photograph of the "not typical" woman, Charlie. Indeed, the two pictures are not just walls apart, but worlds apart. If Charlie strikes out on her own, then she may after all fulfill her mother's own repressed desires and, in doing so, remind us that there is more to a mother's story that needs to be told.

The final horror of the *Santa Rosa Republican*, as Michie rightly shows, is the news of unbearable violence suffered by female victims. For this reason, we may do well to look more carefully not just at what happens when the newspaper passes through Uncle Charlie's hands, but what happens to it when it passes through a woman's hands. To begin this analysis, let us return to the events of the previous night, when Uncle Charlie reads about himself in the evening newspaper. Michie says Uncle Charlie has "appropriated" Joe's paper, though it is important to recall that Emma first appropriates it from her husband, taking it from his hands and in turn giving it to her brother whom she tucks comfortably into the sofa with the words, "There now, lead a life of luxury." Joe and Herb leave the living room and go outside on the front porch to continue their ongoing discussion about the perfect murder. When we return inside, we appear to be alone with Uncle Charlie. He lifts the paper up, obscuring from us the look on his face when he reads the incriminating story. A billowing cloud of smoke emerges from behind the newspaper, which slowly falls away to reveal Uncle Charlie's face. He looks about the room and sees only his niece Ann, who is not sitting on but kneeling before a chair, upon which her book rests comfortably. She is facing away from him, so there is no reason why Uncle Charlie can't quietly excuse himself and take care of the newspaper elsewhere, in a discrete manner. Instead, he calls Ann over and asks her if she's ever seen a house made out of newspapers. She stands next to him, visibly unimpressed. Luckily for her, it takes Uncle Charlie only ten seconds to complete it. Like the telescopic newspaper in *Marnie*, the *Santa Rosa Republican* seems to have a magic of its own. It becomes a house instantly.

But Uncle Charlie isn't done yet: he tears off a small piece of newspaper, which is the incriminating story about him. As he does so, he says "rip the door . . . right off." Now we have a house with no door. And if this is meant to be the Newton home, or any home for that matter, there needs to be a door. Without one, anyone may gain inside access. This seems to be a pointless exercise—particularly for Uncle Charlie. After all, it is he who, only moments later in the film, scolds his sister for allowing strangers in the house: "I'm just a visitor here," he sternly tells Emma, "and my advice to you is to slam the door in his face." Of course, it's very likely the police detectives will find a way into the Newton home door or no door (and so will Herb). The important point here is this: Uncle Charlie thinks he can disappear in Santa Rosa. But he can't. His visit is, after all, big news—and not just to the Newton family. His fame is what makes Uncle Charlie's newspaper game so peculiar. His aim is to rid the newspaper of an incriminating story, to make himself disappear from its headlines; but in doing so, he makes the newspaper, and himself, the center of attention.

And he won't stop. Roger enters the room, and before the boy can cry out "you've got papa's paper!" Uncle Charlie has already presented it to him, but this time as a "nice, little red barn." The more changes the newspaper undergoes, the more eyes are on it. Now Charlie enters the room and, sure enough, the first thing she notices is the newspaper, whose sheets are on the table, strewn upon the floor, folded and torn apart. Despite Uncle Charlie's efforts, the newspaper is now very much on Charlie's mind. And for the next several sequences in the film, it is very much in her hands. Moments after Uncle Charlie's "little game," we see her climbing the stairs carrying a tray with a bottle of water and a glass. She walks to her bedroom, where her Uncle is staying, and knocks on the door. Unbeknownst to Charlie, this scene has happened before, when Uncle Charlie's landlady knocks on the door at the beginning of the film. Then, as now, he replies with a faint "come in." And we should be reminded that it was in this scene we first saw a newspaper, close to a bottle of water and some glasses, and wads of too much cash. One could say that Charlie's knowledge at last coincides with ours: there's something in that newspaper that Uncle Charlie is hiding. She sets down the water and, turning to leave, spots the missing pages of newspaper in her uncle's jacket. "Well now I know there was something in the evening paper about you," she tells him. Uncle Charlie calmly says she's right, that there was something in the evening paper he didn't want anyone to know about, a story about someone he used to know. Charlie impulsively grabs the newspaper from her uncle's jacket and, proudly unfolding it, declares, "There!" But there is no "there" there. Uncle Charlie has ripped the story out, leaving a gaping hole behind. So there is no reason Charlie would dispute anything her uncle might say to fill the hole in. But rather than put the matter to rest with a simple explanation, Uncle Charlie leaps at his niece and grabs her violently by the wrists. After regaining his composure, Uncle Charlie resumes his little game: he tries to deflect attention away from the newspaper, only to ensure Charlie's growing interest in it. His last words before he says good night to her are "Not for you to read . . . forget it."

The words, of course, have the opposite effect: the story *is* for her to read, and she will not forget that newspaper. In fact, she will not let go of it. After returning home after a long and troubling talk with Detective Jack Graham, the first thing she does is search for the missing pages of newspaper. She finds the pages ripped apart and crumpled up at the bottom of a trashcan and takes them back to her sister's room, which she has been sharing during Uncle Charlie's visit, and places them on her bed. When Ann asks Charlie what she is doing, Charlie tells her she is looking for a recipe. Ann replies, "They have papers in the library, new ones and old ones. Miss Cochran will get them out for you. She won't even notice if you cut out a little bitty recipe." Ann is wrong to think, as Charlie no longer does, that something about a newspaper can pass unnoticed or be forgotten. But Ann is right to point her sister in the direction of the library, where newspapers are on full and very public display. (I'll return shortly to the importance of the library as a "public" place.) The camera follows Charlie as she races down the steps of the back stairway and begins her desperate flight to the public library, which is about to close, and we see her clutch the pieces of newspaper in her hands, twisting them ever more tightly into a ball. As she makes her way through the surprisingly crowded streets of Santa Rosa (this is no sleepy little town), the ball of crumpled up newspaper is still visible, if only barely, in her hand. I am certain she still grips it as she weaves her way through traffic in the next few shots, but less certain it is in her hands when she finally arrives at the steps of the library. When she reaches the front door, she spreads both hands on the glass. Her newspaper has somehow vanished.

Inside the empty library, however, Charlie will find her newspaper replaced and restored among dozens of other city newspapers, stacked upon each other in shelves and neatly draped along newspaper sticks. She lifts a few of these sticks, then turns to the shelves to find what would be the *Santa Rosa Republican*, yesterday's evening edition. She sits herself down at a table and scans through its pages. What follows is one of the most extraordinary shots in the film: the close-up of the missing headline, "Where is the Merry Widow Murderer?" The dramatic crescendo of Dmitri Tiomkin's score adds a good deal of drama to this newspaper's "entrance," but more striking is the extremity of the close-up. For much of the film, we strain our eyes to read the *Santa Rosa Republican*. Now it seems almost too close. This shot is, in fact, the first of three extreme close-ups in the film, all of which can be linked: the second is the one that ends Uncle Charlie's frightening monologue about "faded, fat, greedy women," and the third is the one of the ring on Charlie's finger as she descends the stairs near the end of the film. Taken together, the three extreme close-ups virtually close the case: the headline tells us that the ring ties Uncle Charlie to the murder; the dolly in to an extreme-close up of the ring shows that it is now in Charlie's hands; the extreme close-up of Uncle Charlie answers the headline's question: the Merry Widow murderer is right here in the Newton house.

What remains open, however, is the question of what happened to that piece of crumpled newspaper Charlie was holding tightly—so much so that it is hard to imagine it slipped from her fingers on her way to the public library. It is a question I do not think is easily dismissed, for example, as a negligible continuity error. One answer, which only seems dismissive, is that Charlie doesn't need those pieces of newspaper. They do her about as much good as it did Uncle Charlie to rip them out in the first place. The *Santa Rosa Republican* is a city newspaper; where there is one copy, there are ten thousand or more. What Charlie finds in the public library is not only yesterday's edition of the *Santa Rosa Republican*, but dozens of other city papers. And if we associate the newspaper with the crowd, as I have been arguing that we should, we might say that the culmination of Charlie's search for the truth about her uncle takes place in a crowd of newspapers. Indeed, not since *The Lodger* have so many newspapers appeared at once, in a single shot, in a Hitchcock film. It's not surprising, then, that Hitchcock would crowd the streets of Santa Rosa during Charlie's flight to the public library. Looking carefully at the sequence, we see the streets teeming with people. The idea for crowding downtown Santa Rosa was not simply to create obstacles for Charlie, in the way Hitchcock did for little Stevie in the infamous bomb sequence in *Sabotage* (1936). By doing so, Hitchcock *does* create suspense (will Charlie get to the library in time?). But he also reminds us of the newspaper's ties to the city. Joe Newton's newspaper may be an emblem of domestic tranquility (under threat, of course) but only when we see it at home. When Charlie runs to the public library, carrying pieces of the newspaper, we are reminded that the *Santa Rosa Republican* is also a city paper, a very public thing, and an emblem of the modern, urban crowd. We are also reminded that, for all his talk about the good old days of small town Santa Rosa, Uncle Charlie is a modern, urban killer.

*   *   *   *   *   *

I wish to conclude this discussion of Hitchcock's newspaper, that conspicuous thing in the crowd, by re-emphasizing its close association with the cinema, and with Hitchcock's camera in particular. Given this close association, we should pay particular attention to those moments in his films in which a newspaper is present. I'd like to close with a brief discussion of *The Lodger*, not simply to insist that Hitchcock's interest in crowd/newspaper/cinema was there at the outset, but to suggest that no other Hitchcock film gives us a clearer example of this rich and strange figuration. Let's begin with the scene in which the policeman, Joe Chandler (Malcolm Keen), discovers a valise belonging to the lodger, locked in a dresser drawer. In this valise, he finds several items that seem to confirm his suspicion that the lodger is the serial killer known as the Avenger: a pistol, a map of the murders (which Joe calls "a plan of the murders"), several newspaper clippings, and a portrait of a beautiful, fair-haired girl. What is most striking about this moment in the film is that Joe seems especially troubled by the newspaper clippings.

Hitchcock's camera lingers the longest on a small collection of clippings from the *Evening Standard*. No less circumstantial than the other items, these newspaper clippings nevertheless all but confirm the lodger's guilt in Joe's mind. To be sure, Joe has discovered what Charlie could never find until her flight to the public library: the truth in print. And whereas Charlie beheld only one breathtaking headline, Joe takes in several. Taken together, these headlines create the film's second quasi-documentary (the first being the sequence which opens the film). With compelling sequential logic, we see, writ large, the story of *The Lodger* itself: "Stabbed. Murdered in Brother's Arms at Coming-out Ball. Avenger Triangle Clue. Work of a Maniac? Third Avenger Murder. Fair-haired Waitress Killed at Charing Cross Station. Police Clues Fail. Avenger Still at Large."

What follows is a striking demonstration of the effect this mini-documentary has on Joe. We see him in close-up, standing bent over the table, his face hidden by his fedora. As he slowly turns his head to the right, the fedora continues to mask his face. Finally, Joe lifts his head and reveals to us a look of unshakable resolve: he will name the lodger the Avenger. Yet even without the knowledge revealed in a subsequent flashback, there is every reason to believe that Joe is dead wrong; and it is with Joe's next gesture that we can appreciate the lodger's growing sense of utter hopelessness. Joe pulls one final item from the valise, the portrait of a beautiful, fair-haired girl. "Your first victim, eh?" he says.

The lodger's response, "My murdered sister," connects by association to the first headline of the *Evening Standard* that Joe reads. So why does Joe get it so wrong? In his reading of this scene, Rothman raises the question that is at the heart of not only *The Lodger*, but the world of Hitchcock's films: "can innocence be recognized? If so, by whom and under what circumstances, and how are we to account for the fact that the guilty routinely pass for innocent and the innocent for guilty in Hitchcock's world as in our world?"[21] But there is something else going on here, something else besides the blindness of love (and the blindness of jealousy) that causes the misrecognition of innocence and guilt in the world of Hitchcock. It is as if the newspaper clippings do more than engender the contagion of suspicion in the lodger; they induce in Joe what might be called a "crowd mentality." This is why he says, after he learns of the lodger's innocence, "Quick— before they tear him to pieces!" Joe thinks like the crowd, knows that the newspaper creates the crowd, fuels it and sustains it.

Hitchcock depicts the full force of this crowd mentality early in *The Lodger*. The film opens with the sequence of shots that follow the lights that three times flash, "*TO–NIGHT `GOLDEN CURLS.'* " The body of a young woman is seen lying on the street. We then see an old woman, a witness to the murder, describing the man whom we will learn moments later is the Avenger. A few shots later, we see the journalist racing into a phone booth. A crowd has gathered around a coffee stand, where the old woman, now revived by a cup of tea, describes the murderer by placing her hand over her face, just below the eyes: "Tall he was— and his face all wrapped up," she recalls. As a joke, a man standing in the nearby crowd pulls his coat over his face, mimicking the old woman's description. She sees his face, a spitting image of the murderer she has just described, reflected on the coffee stand's shiny steel container. The old woman screams, and the prankster is scolded. The next shot is of the journalist in a phone booth, furiously dictating the story, which is then telegraphed, printed, and sent out to the newspaper-reading public. Thus in a long sequence of shots comprising what Rothman describes as a "quasi-documentary," a series of textual relays is established: through the telephone, to the newspaper office, onto a telegraph device, through the printing presses onto news sheets, into trucks and onto crowded streets, across a news ticker and through the crowd, and finally over the radio. From this "quasi-documentary," Rothman singles out what he calls "three characteristic touches":

> First, Hitchcock personally appears as an extra in an editorial office. (He appears again at the film's climax.) Second, as a truck carrying bales of newspapers drives into the depths of the frame, two heads, visible through oval windows, swing back and forth . . . as though they were the newspaper van's eyes. Third, a crowd is shown looking upward, all eyes moving in unison—to all appearances, an audience viewing a film. . . . When Hitchcock cuts to the crowd's point of view, we realize that these people are reading a huge electric sign spelling out the *Evening Standard*'s report of the latest Avenger murder.[22]

Rothman's argument here is that the newspaper reading public's appetite for murder is what draws them to Hitchcock's film.[23] More broadly, one might argue that the opening sequence of *The Lodger* shows us that, in a sense, the crowd is always already at the movies. By Rothman's account, what precedes the "quasi documentary" of textual relays is mere reportage or word of mouth. Yet before the journalist has a chance to send the description of the Avenger to the *Evening Standard* office, the old woman in the crowd sees it projected *on a silver screen*. The hidden face of the Avenger is already making its way through crowds. Perhaps this is what Rothman tries to suggest after all, for Hitchcock's aim here is to "plant the image of the Avenger in the spectator's mind," therefore making it almost impossible to discriminate between the innocent and the guilty.[26] As Gustave Le Bon, who gave us the first study of the psychology of the modern, urban crowd, writes:

> A crowd thinks in images, and the image itself immediately calls up a series of other images, having no logical connection with the first. We can easily conceive this state by thinking of the fantastic succession of ideas to which we are sometimes led by calling up in our minds any fact. Our reason shows us the incoherence there is in these images, but a crowd is almost blind to this truth, and confuses with the real event what the deforming action of its imagination has superimposed thereon.[25]

One can easily associate what Le Bon describes in the above passage with a typical evening at the Lumière *cinématographe*, where the spectator perceives a series of images calling up another series, with no logical connection from one to the next—a succession of "views" that the spectator, through the deforming action of his or her imagination, may confuse with the real event (an arrival of a train at the station, for instance). Indeed, what is most striking about the above passage is not the swift and suspect manner in which the crowd is condemned (as scholars of crowd psychology have noted, the success of Le Bon's work "is attributable more to his way with aphorism than to rigorous sociological analysis").[26] Rather, it is the proto-cinematic power that Le Bon reluctantly grants the crowd, which is not only assembled by purveyors of images but itself has the power to assemble images, and to superimpose itself upon them as well.

If we find the crowd to be a most peculiar of Hitchcock propensities, it is because the Hitchcock crowd so frequently exploits the power Le Bon here describes. The Hitchcock crowd is not only assembled by movies but is itself a "movie machine"; it conjures images of itself and, with its most

Figure 10

trusted purveyor, the newspaper, conspires to expose us all. This strange but telling figuration that I have been calling "crowd/newspaper/cinema" is captured wonderfully in *North by Northwest* (figure 10) in a frame conjoining a crowd (the faces on Mt. Rushmore), a newspaper (which the Professor holds in his hands), and cinema (the optic device through which Thornhill looks). And as I have argued, this figuration appears throughout Hitchcock's works. Indeed, once we choose to follow the newspaper on its tangled journey from *The Lodger* to that film's distant cousin, *Frenzy!* (1972), we are not much surprised to discover that the Hitchcock landscape is overcrowded with media, but struck with a feeling most uncanny that it is over-mediated by the crowd.

Notes

1. Ink with graphite under drawing. Signed b.r. "Phil May 96." 26.7 x 15.5 com., 10-7/16 x 6-1/8" sheet. Lent Courtesy of Private Collection. Reprinted in *Origins of Modernity*, ed. Catherine Carter Goebel (Rock Island, IL: Augustana College, 2005), 155.

2. Philip Fisher, *Still the New World: American Literature in a Culture of Creative Destruction* (Cambridge: Harvard University Press, 1999), 251. This idea is echoed by David M. Henkin, who draws an equally explicit link between the newspaper format and

the crowd: "Discrete news stories, tendentious political commentaries, competitive commercial claims, and ostensibly unrelated bits of information blended together in the print columns of the metropolitan press in a characteristically urban juxtaposition of unlikely neighbors that also imbued all of the texts with the appearance of sharing a single, impersonal authority." See *City Reading: Written Words and Public Spaces in Antebellum New York* (New York: Columbia University Press, 1998), 119.

3. It is worth noting that out of all of Hitchcock's cameos, four of them involve newspapers: in the first, Hitchcock appears as a newspaper editor (*The Lodger* [1926]); in both *Foreign Correspondent* (1940) and *Stage Fright* (1950) he appears reading a newspaper; in the fourth, he is pictured in a newspaper (*Lifeboat* [1944]). One may further speculate that in his cameo in *Young and Innocent* (1937), Hitchcock appears as a photographer who works for a newspaper, which would in fact bring the total number of newspaper-related cameos to five.

4. There are objects of significance that appear in more than one Hitchcock film, such as the key in both *Notorious* and *Dial M for Murder* and the ring in both *Shadow of a Doubt* and *Rear Window*. Yet neither of these objects has the busy itinerary of Hitchcock's newspaper. Sarah Street's insightful essay, "Hitchcockian Haberdashery" (in *Framing Hitchcock: Selected Essays from the Hitchcock Annual*, ed. Sidney Gottlieb and Christopher Brookhouse [Detroit: Wayne State University Press, 2002], 147-58) draws our attention to another busy Hitchcockian object: the woman's handbag. Like the newspaper, the handbag is given "consistent, obtrusive visual attention" in several films (147). What makes the newspaper a more prominent object is not that it appears in far more films (Street sees the handbag as essential only in films made during the years 1954-64) but that its meaning, its function, its very shape is always changing. To be sure, the Hitchcock handbag is a focal enough object to be worthy of study, but it is an unchanging visual symbol: of "the threat of secrets or independent female identity" (151). For a fuller inventory of significant objects in Hitchcock's films, see Michael Walker, *Hitchcock's Motifs* (Amsterdam: Amsterdam University Press, 2006), 343.

5. Ina Rae Hark, "'We Might Even Get in the Newsreels'": The Press and Democracy in Hitchcock's World War II Anti-Fascist Films," in *Alfred Hitchcock: Centenary Essays*, ed. Richard Allen and S. Ishii Gonzáles (London: BFI Publishing, 1999), 335.

6. Hark, "'We Might Even Get in the Newsreels,'" 334.

7. Ned Schantz, *Gossip, Letters, Phones: The Scandal of Female Networks in Film and Literature* (New York: Oxford University Press, 2008), 56.

8. William Rothman, *Hitchcock: The Murderous Gaze* (Cambridge: Harvard University Press, 1981). Mel Brooks, in his parody of Hitchcock's films, *High Anxiety* (1977), takes the idea of the murderous newspaper literally. The psychiatrist Richard H. Thorndyke (Brooks) is waiting impatiently for a newspaper, which he had requested several times from a hotel bellboy. In a hilarious take on the shower scene from *Psycho*, the newspaper is finally delivered. Shrieking hysterically, the bellboy stabs Thorndyke repeatedly with the rolled-up newspaper. Stunned, Thorndyke collapses in the tub as the newspaper ink washes down the drain.

9. The films in which the newspaper can be considered a prominent and recurrent object are *The Lodger*, *Champagne* (1928), *Blackmail* (1929), *Rich and Strange* (1931), *The 39 Steps* (1935), *The Lady Vanishes* (1939), *Foreign Correspondent* (1940), *Shadow of a Doubt* (1943), *Lifeboat*, *North by Northwest* (1959), *Psycho* (1960), and *Marnie* (1964). But the newspaper is an important object in other films as well, frequently tied to a character's presumed (if sometimes mistaken) guilt. In *Strangers on a Train*, it is not clear if Bruno recognizes Guy because he's seen him in the sports section of the newspaper or its society pages—given Bruno's polymorphous perversity, it is most likely both. After the opening sequence of *To Catch a Thief* (1955), in which a woman's scream is followed by a shot of a black cat prowling the rooftops, we find ourselves in the estate of John Robie. We see a cleaning woman tidying up, and then the image shifts to a shot of a black cat, lying on top of a newspaper. A close-up of the paper shows a story, "The Cat Prowls Again?" written by Art Buchwald. In *The Complete Films of Alfred Hitchcock* (New York: Citadel Press, 2002), 171, Robert A. Harris and Michael S. Lasky note that there are claw marks slashed through this story. But the claw marks are in the column to the right (both columns fall under the heading "Europe's Lighter Side") in which Buchwald describes the difficulties that television personalities have in writing off their expenses when traveling to Europe. The story recalls the film's title shot of a window of a travel agency—a shot that will be virtually repeated early in the title sequence of *North by Northwest*. In *The Wrong Man* (1956), we see that Manny Ballestrero likes to read the racing pages of the newspaper and pick the winning horses—a

hobby that, as Paula Marantz Cohen rightly claims, marks Manny as a potential criminal from the start (see *Alfred Hitchcock: the Legacy of Victorianism* [Lexington, KY: University of Kentucky Press, 1995], 127). In *Frenzy*, a newspaper is pushed underneath the door of Babs's apartment, as Blaney sleeps in her bed. On the front page is a story about yet another necktie murder. In the following shot, we see Babs's landlord reading the same story, in which a perfect description of Blaney is given. This sequence is perhaps the culmination of a whole career devoted to putting heroes wrongly accused on the front page.

10. I am nevertheless encouraged to take this next step, not simply because of the growing scholarly interest in "thing theory" in general, but because an interest in Hitchcock's "things" is a long-standing one. Although much overstated, Jean-Luc Godard's point, made in Toronto during a 1996 interview with Jonathan Rosenbaum, is clear: "And something which is very astonishing with Hitchcock is that you don't remember what the story of *Notorious* is, or why Janet Leigh is going to the Bates Motel. You remember one pair of spectacles or a windmill—that's what millions and millions of people remember. If you remember *Notorious*, what do you remember? Wine bottles. You don't remember Ingrid Bergman. When you remember Griffith or Welles or Eisenstein or me, you don't remember ordinary objects. He is the only one." Jonathan Rosenbaum, "Trailer for Godard's *Histoire(s) du Cinema*," *Trafic* 21 (1997), online at http://www.jonathanrosenbaum.com/?p=15760.

11. Even with only two James Bond films released by 1964, contemporaneous audiences of *Marnie*, as well as audiences today, would no doubt be reminded of the opening of every James Bond film, in which Secret Service agent 007 is spied through a gun barrel.

12. Quoted in David Henkin, *City Reading: Written Words and Public Spaces in Antebellum New York* (New York: Columbia University Press, 1998), 109.

13. Frederick Knight Hunt, *The Fourth Estate: Contributions Towards a History of Newspapers, and of the Liberties of the Press, Vol 1.* (London: David Bogue, 1850), 2.

14. Gerald Stanley Lee, *Crowds: A Moving-Picture of Democracy* (New York: Doubleday, Page & Company, 1913), 28.

15. If the stroking inside the hole of the newspaper does not sufficiently suggest that rape is on the minds of the men in *Marnie*, it is important to recall that Hitchcock insisted on including the scene from Winston Graham's novel in which Mark rapes Marnie,

despite the objections of the second of his three screenwriters on the project, Evan Hunter. Although the film itself is full of suggestive references to rape (the red suffusions, the drops of red ink on Marnie's shirt, and so on), it is in the trailer for Hitchcock's film that an explicit connection is made between sexual violence and investigative probing. Over the scene in Mark's office when the thunderstorm hits, Hitchcock delivers a campy voice-over characteristic of his introductions and send-offs from his hit television anthology, *Alfred Hitchcock Presents*. As we see the shot of a tree trunk bursting through the window, Hitchcock says "Marnie's trouble goes deeper than that . . . far deeper." Over a subsequent shot of Mark kissing Marnie, Hitchcock continues: "And this is the problem that Mark must probe."

16. Nor is Roger Thornhill really looking through the binoculars at Mount Rushmore. This bit of deception may account for his odd statement, "I don't like the way Teddy Roosevelt is looking at me." As Stanley Cavell has observed, Roosevelt *isn't* looking at Roger Thornhill. But then again, Thornhill isn't looking at Roosevelt either. See *"North by Northwest,"* in *A Hitchcock Reader*, second edition, ed. Marshall Deutelbaum and Leland Poague (Malden, MA: Wiley-Blackwell, 2011), 250-63.

17. Robin Wood. *Hitchcock's Films Revisited*, revised edition (New York: Columbia University Press, 2002), 45.

18. Elsie B. Michie, "Unveiling Maternal Desires: Hitchcock and American Domesticity," in *Hitchcock's America*, ed. Jonathan Freeman and Richard Millington (New York: Oxford University Press, 1999), 45-46.

19. Michie, "Unveiling Maternal Desires," 46.

20. Michie, "Unveiling Maternal Desires," 37.

21. Rothman, *Hitchcock: The Murderous Gaze,* 40.

22. Rothman, *Hitchcock: The Murderous Gaze*, 9-10.

23. Tom Ryall, citing the work of Alan Lovell, refers to the "the *News of the World* culture" that is portrayed in *The Lodger*, a tabloid newspaper culture from which Hitchcock's cinematic identity derived: "The '*News of the World* culture' with its emphasis on sexuality and violence is a central component of the `strong under-life' of British cinema which runs counter to the `cinema of good taste, characterised by restraint, understatement and sophistication' preferred by the orthodox film culture and it is to the subversive counter-current that Hitchcock's British films relate." See *Alfred Hitchcock and the British Cinema* (London: Athlone Press, 1996), 179.

24. Rothman, *Hitchcock: The Murderous Gaze*, 9-10.

25. Gustav Le Bon, *The Crowd: A Study of the Popular Mind*, 2nd ed. (New York: Macmillan Company, 1897), 22.

26. See Jeffrey T. Schnapp and Matthew Tiews, "Introduction: A Book of Crowds," in *Crowds*, ed. Jeffrey T. Schnapp and Matthew Tiews (Stanford: Stanford University Press, 2006), ix.

DAVID GREVEN

Intimate Violence:
Marnie *and Queer Resilience*

Marnie (1964) is one of Alfred Hitchcock's most important films for several reasons. It is not only the last masterpiece of his greatest period, beginning with his 1956 remake of his earlier *The Man Who Knew Too Much* (1934), and including *The Wrong Man* (1956), *Vertigo* (1958), *North by Northwest* (1959), *Psycho* (1960), and *The Birds* (1963), but is in many ways the culmination of the period in Hitchcock's work that brings his chief concerns into a startling new prominence. These concerns include the hollowness of relationships in capitalist patriarchy; the difficulties of achieving authentic and intimate bonds, both emotional and sexual, primarily between men and women in the narratives, but a question with queer implications as well; the blankness of identity; the increasingly violent war between nature and the human, or the real and the symbolic; and relationships between adult children and their parents, often between the adult and their mother, mothers being an especially vexed figure throughout Hitchcock's work.

In terms of *Marnie*, what is especially relevant about this period as a whole is that it consistently thematizes the figure of the postwar American wife as a representation of women's conflict-ridden relationship to patriarchy. *The Man Who Knew Too Much* (1956) explores, among other subjects, the struggles of the former career woman to accommodate herself to marriage and family and their demands. Similarly, *The Wrong*

Figure 1. The wife and the social setting.

Man treats its own version of what Freud called "the housewife's psychosis," where the central drama of the film is not the story of the wrongfully imprisoned man but, instead, his wife's increasing instability and descent into madness as a result of the strains of her husband's attempts to exonerate himself. The heroine of *Marnie* is in many ways a former career woman—criminality her profession—similarly chafing against the demands of marriage, and threatening to descend into madness. The "wife" is an unstable category in which to "contain" femininity, but a serviceable category through which to register the woman's gendered anxieties as well as conflictual desires. Most vividly, the films represent the condition of femininity as one of entrapment: brilliantly allegorized in the close-up of Doris Day's Jo McKenna, utterly overwhelmed and alone with her unbearable decision whether or not to cry out and stop the assassination at the risk of losing her child in *The Man Who Knew Too Much*; in the discussion in *Psycho* between Norman Bates (Anthony Perkins) and Marion Crane (Janet Leigh) about maddening and inescapable private traps; in the literal entrapment of Melanie Daniels (Tippi Hedren) in the telephone booth, a flimsy defense against the titular birds; and throughout *Marnie*, where marriage is the ultimate trap for capturing the truly "wild" woman (as pictured, for example, in fig. 1). Hitchcock's analysis of the figure of the wife finds archetypal realization in *Vertigo*, with its protagonist's central obsession with another man's wife, who herself appears to be obsessed with an ancestral woman who could not be another man's wife.

In these films, marriage, the comedic climax of narrative that promises renewal and fertility, comes to seem like its opposite, a death-like nullity. The death-obsession of *Vertigo* finds an apposite complement in *North by Northwest*, as Hitchcock eerily blurs the line between near-death experience and marriage in the final scenes: the dream-like transition of the couple from the precarious verge of death to marriage, signified by the exultant line, "Come along, *Mrs. Thornhill*," as Roger O. Thornhill (Cary Grant) lifts Eve Kendall (Eva Marie Saint) into his upper train berth in a Pullman car. Marion Crane wants marriage enough to wreck her life over it. That her shocking shower murder occurs despite her attempt to pick up the pieces of her self-sabotaged life and return the stolen money is just one of the film's unspeakably grim ironies. *Marnie* builds on the strains over marital roles and the woman's difficulties in marriage in these films, deepening their resonances and political implications to the point of almost unendurable poignancy. As I will show, one of the effects of the focus on the wife or wife-like woman is to cast the heterosexual male lead into relief as a newly available object of desire—and dread.

At the same time, *Marnie* reflects a new maturity in the director's treatment of one his recurring and most vexed themes: the cold, remote mother who either withholds her affection from her child or smothers the child in overwhelmingly intense need. If *Psycho* transforms this deep ambivalence over mother-child relationships into the stuff of nightmares (captured vividly in that indelible shot of Norman over which the dead mother's skull-face is superimposed and her chilling words preside), *The Birds* evinces the development of some sympathy for the ambivalent mother's position as well as that of the wayward, disoriented modern daughter. *Marnie* treats maternal ambivalence, both the mother's expression of it and the child's experience of it, with palpable emotional intensity. In one shot of the mother in silhouette going down the stairs, her descent punctuated by the echoing footsteps of a bad dream, we are back in *Psycho* territory of the maternal uncanny; by the end of the film, the mother is all too pitiably and recognizably a lonely, defeated, human figure. Finally, *Marnie* extends the extraordinary formal experimentation that marks this period of Hitchcock's work, especially apparent before *Marnie* in *Vertigo* (with its brooding long takes, experiments with symbolic color, multi-media dream sequence combining live-action with animation, and exploded and restarted narrative, which also influences *Psycho*) and *The Birds* (with Hitchcock's unprecedented use of special effects and the film's brazenly allegorical style and structure). While denigrated, especially in its initial release, for its supposed aesthetic failures, *Marnie* is, as I hope to convey, one of Hitchcock's most daringly conceived films in formal terms that, at every point, match its content.

Queer Resilience, Class, and Anti-Relationality

Marnie is one of the cinema's richest explorations of what I call *queer resilience*: a continuous level of self-reliance and fortitude within structures of stifling social conformity that emphasize visible manifestations of gender and sexual normativity—being properly male or female, on the one hand, and on the other, being manifestly and unimpeachably heterosexual, an achievement most commonly confirmed by marriage. The social order as *Marnie* envisions it not only depends on but also promulgates constriction, loneliness, and an inexorable descent into violation and violence, which frequently occurs within the most intimate bonds (e.g., mother-child, the married couple). The forms of intimate violence that Hitchcock's films frequently depict find a newly politicized urgency in *Marnie*. Marnie's queer resilience can be described as her constant effort to stay alive (save when she feels forced to attempt suicide) and to derive some form of pleasure and satisfaction from the experience of staying alive in a culture that negates, through its deeply focused and specific demands, the heroine's very means of existing. Queer resilience is conveyed in the moments of the film in which Marnie seems to be deriving genuine pleasure from her life despite the costs of achieving that pleasure, to say nothing of enduring such a life. Queer resilience also comes through in, or informs, the numerous, indeed, the defining, moments in which Marnie appears abject and victimized.

My argument considers the relationship of the overarching theme of isolation to the concerns with sex, gender, and class that are central to the film. I will offer close readings of certain key scenes—in particular the fox-hunt sequence and the controversial shipboard sex/rape scene, and also the thunderstorm in Mark Rutland's office, Marnie's attempted theft of Mark's money after the fox-hunt, and the climax, with its flashback to the scene of Marnie's (and her mother's) "primal" trauma—to make my theoretical claims more lucid. The longstanding vexed questions about *Marnie*'s aesthetic worth strangely mirror the centrally vexed question of personal worth in its heroine.

Important readings of the film as a thematization of lesbian desire have been offered. While my interpretation builds on these, I am specifically using the term "queer" here for its broader political associations as a stance taken against heteronormative structures of society and social commonplaces such as heterosexual presumption. Fascinating overlaps exist between the film's concerns and those of contemporary queer theory. The film's critique of sexual politics in capitalism dovetails with queer theory's reconsideration of class and Marxist theory, as evinced by a recent special issue of *GLQ* entitled "Queer Studies and the Crises of Capitalism."[1] We can also understand *Marnie* as an exploration of the "anti-relationality" thesis. Marnie's various methods of eschewing or remaining remote from social relationships evoke the concept of anti-relationality, derived from the writings of Jean Genet, in the work of Leo Bersani and Lee Edelman. The premise of these theoreticians' argument is that, instead of accommodating straight culture's demands and conforming to heteronormative standards, queer subjects might more profitably resist the social altogether, remaining, but purposefully so, outside the social mainstream.[2]

Marnie does, indeed, seem to pursue an anti-relational approach to life, treating the social in many respects as a game in which she participates only in a knowing, detached, uninvested manner. The joke would always seem to be on the social realm, in her view. But what the film offers—which queer theory does not, in my opinion, offer—is an analysis of the emotional costs of anti-relationity, as well as the subject's own investments in the world and in relationships, however ambivalent these may be. Marnie's reliance on reserves of personal strength in the face of crushing social demands that seem to begin and end with the normatively sexual is valuable to an understanding of queer sexuality in Hitchcock's work. While the anti-relational thesis may illuminate certain aspects of her struggle, what it does not illuminate is her struggle itself, the ways in which grappling with the social order provokes conflicted, push-pull feelings in her that suggestively indicate the nature of maintaining an actively resistant stance toward the social order.

The "social" as imagined by the film is an extraordinarily intricate realm of constrictions on every level, modes of existence to which the individual is pressured to conform, an endless series of demands, and an overarching hierarchy of established values that then govern all interactions among social actors ("acting" being a crucial, multivalent trope here). Normative sexual desire—which is to say, institutionalized and compulsory heterosexual desire—emerges as the organizing principle of the social, the logic of all relationships and motivations. Conforming to, maintaining, and, to evoke Judith Butler, *achieving* a normative sexual desire and life becomes the visible, verifiable marker that one is indeed a "normal" functioning person and that one has not only conformed to but is also able to embody a prescribed gender role. As Butler writes, "masculine and feminine are not dispositions, as Freud sometimes argues, but indeed accomplishments, ones which emerge in tandem with the achievement of heterosexuality."[3] This gender and sexual normalcy—which I call *visual identity*, an outward manifestation of one's properly achieved conformity to and successful embodiment of this normalcy— intersects, as the film shows, with other social demands and standards by which the individual is relentlessly and routinely judged. In *Marnie*, as perhaps in life, these demands are organized around class. This is not to say that other organizing structures, such as race, especially, do not also wield

Figure 2. Lil's desire for Marnie.

considerable power, but that, arguably, class hierarchy undergirds other forms of prejudice, such as racism and homophobia, and, perhaps, sexism/misogyny as well.

Camp and drag—topics that lend themselves to the fluctuating tonal registers of the film and the remarkable series of costume and hairstyle changes on display—could be described as forms of queer resilience as well. Clearly, Marnie's resilience cannot be confused with the ability to transcend her situation or parody it into an alternative mode of pleasure; it is neither camp nor drag. At the same time, it is remarkable how often Marnie seems to explore the forms of drag, female as well as male: the succession of outfits from her Athena-like dress at the party where she re-encounters Strutt to her cat burglar outfit immediately after the party, intertextually evoking Cary Grant's "The Cat" in *To Catch a Thief* (1955).

Lesbian Desire

Lucretia Knapp has read *Marnie* as a specifically lesbian film, focusing—as Raymond Bellour in his determinedly heterosexist schemas decidedly does not, on the female relationships in the film, most notably between Marnie (Tippi Hedren) and Lil Mainwaring (Diana Baker), who eyes the new girl Marnie as she suggestively remarks to Mark Rutland (Sean Connery), "Who's the dish?" (fig. 2).[4] Knapp also discusses Marnie's relationship with Susan Clabon, the warm, kind, smiling fellow secretary at Rutland's (played by Mariette Hartley, quietly superb as always). Without diminishing the welcome lesbian specificity of Knapp's reading, I want to make a broader case for Marnie as a queer character whose queerness stems, paradoxically, from her refusals of sexuality and female friendship.

Knapp's discussion of the relationship between Marnie and Lil emphasizes Lil as Marnie's "protector, comforter, and sympathizer."[5] It is interesting to note that in the source material for Hitchcock's film, Winston Graham's *Marnie*, an English novel first published in 1961, there is no "Lil" character but rather a gay man named Terry Holbrook, frequently described as "bitchy." I believe that Lil is a deliciously polymorphously-perverse character, especially as wittily played by the dark-haired, tartly poised Baker. She seems equally aroused by Marnie and her sexual possibilities as well as her brother-in-law Mark and his inaccessible handsomeness. But while Lil does seem to come to Marnie's aid when Forio is grievously injured and does offer her comfort as she lies in bed after her nightmare, she is primarily a "negative" character, the wicked dark lady to Marnie's vulnerable fair lady, vengefully inviting Strutt to the post-wedding party that Mark throws for Marnie and that is Marnie's big social "coming out." In this manner, Lil more than links up to the malevolent Mrs. Danvers in *Rebecca* (1940)—a film that is an important intertext for *Marnie*—who successfully tricks the heroine into dressing up in the same dress (worn by a female de Winter ancestor in a family portrait) that Rebecca (secretly hated by Maxim de Winter) wore for the masquerade ball.

To overemphasize the emotional, nurturing links between Lil and Marnie—as opposed to the erotic *frisson* between them—blunts the forcefulness of the film's social critique. Marnie is as constitutionally opposed to same-gender friendships as she is to normative heterosexual relations. Both friendship and heterosexuality are social obligations—markers of the properly socialized and, indeed, the human—even as they are social possibilities.[6] Marnie is a poignant, affecting, sympathetic character precisely because of her aloneness and her despair.[7] Marnie attempts to create a separate, singular reality in which she will be able to fend off the social order's binding demands of friendship and marriage. If true friendship is largely unthinkable in this film—though there are some tender buds of a developing relationship between Marnie and Susan—heterosexual relations are a source and site of pain, violation, betrayal, and violence.

Friendless Marnie has neither mate nor, really, mother.[8] In some respects, Marnie evokes the lonely Norman Bates, not just in terms of mother issues but also in the deep, abiding isolation of their lives. Yet it is also true that before her marriage Marnie is depicted as very much a less abject figure than Norman. While her criminality constricts her life to the point of unlivability, it also, for a time, gives her precisely the freedom for unfeigned self-pleasure and self-society she craves above everything else except the relationship with her mother, which she does just about anything to maintain.

While not wholly indifferent to Marnie, her mother, Mrs. Bernice Edgar (Louise Latham), much more demonstrably and effortlessly bestows her affections on the neighbor's daughter whom she babysits, the blonde girl Jessie. The mother's own conflicted feelings as well as the memory of sexual trauma that she shares with her own child block her from expressing her love for and to her daughter. The heroine's relationship with her mother crucially reveals her isolation. As William Rothman puts it, Marnie is a film of "unbearable sadness," which stems from the thematic of loneliness and withheld love and affection.[9] Hitchcock's frequent depictions of cold, remote mothers take on both a new intensity and a new depth in this film that seeps into the entire narrative. The near inability of the heroine to get her mother's love metonymically represents her entire relationship to the social order.

The film frequently and palpably conveys Marnie's loneliness, most affectingly in the shots that isolate her even when she is in contact with, or at least physical proximity to, others: when, as business shuts down for the day, she hides in the bathroom stall at Rutland's, preparing to steal the money in the safe, as the chatter of the cheerfully loquacious office workers gradually dies down; when Mark, as they stand together inside the stables on his estate, makes suggestive noises to her about their apparently burgeoning romance. In each of these shots, especially the latter, Marnie's expression conveys a deep sense of detachment from what's happening around and to her. It should be added that detachment as it informs such moments is not necessarily a shattering experience; indeed, Marnie, especially in the bathroom stall, seems quite calm and strategic. Marnie's self-sufficiency, even if in a criminal register that makes it untenable, is inextricable from her ambiguous isolation and is a part of her resilience. Separating herself from others might also be a useful refuge from heterosexual demands. For example, an attitude of detachment seems to be what allows Marnie to maintain her studied composure in the stables. But, to be sure, separation transforms into unbearable loneliness: in the scenes between Marnie and her mother; when Marnie breaks down, brittleness giving way to a flood of feeling, as she says "Oh, God, somebody help me"; and in the moment when Marnie cannot grab the money in the Rutland house safe.

The Crime of Onan: Sex and Isolation in Modern Urban Life

Clearly, Marnie struggles with questions of self-worth even as she exudes personal resources for coping with an inhospitable world shown to be as barren, at its heart, as her own spirit must be much of the time. Marnie constructs a shadow world of artifice, a world in which immoral deeds procure transitory and ambiguous pleasures: stolen money is used to buy gifts for an emotionally remote mother, clearly with the intention of pleasing this mother and thereby getting some appreciation and affection from her; and rides on a horse bought with the same illicit funds are made to function as a means of liberation. What is especially curious and

Figure 3. Marnie and Mama.

unsettling here, however, is that the "real" world of the film is depicted in no less artificial, shadowy terms. The vast Rutland building where Marnie works is a towering and imperious structure, imbued with a denatured, fable-like irreality. Visually depicted through a matte painting, the immense building seems almost entirely isolated, existing in a stylized realm all of its own. Mark's mansion, in which he installs Marnie as his wife, is presided over by a man he calls his father (Alan Napier) who has no more intimate connection to him than, say, a fellow businessman might. Irreality and the lack of intimacy in human relationships suggest a blank, denatured world, yet perhaps this world is simply the social order laid bare before us, unvarnished, revealed.[10] But intimacy, as I will show, is not really any better, fraught, as it is, with potential menace.

Marnie seems to mean it when she says to her mother, "We don't need men, Mama. We can do very well ourselves, you and me" (fig. 3). The alternative mother-daughter world Marnie attempts to nurture provides a break from social reality. But it is shown to be a deeply frustrating aspect of the heroine's life that leaves her bereft. Like the hard, isolate, stoic men of classic American literature, Marnie would rather go it alone. In *Vertigo*, the theme of aloneness, even within friendship, significantly emerges in the first scene between Scottie (James Stewart) and Midge (Barbara Bel Geddes) in her apartment, after Scottie has discovered, through a terrifying episode that led to a police

Figure 4. Scottie: a study in frustration.

Figure 5. Midge's concern for Scottie.

officer's death, that he suffers from vertigo. Both Scottie and Midge are presented as sophisticated dwellers of the modern urban world and as friends with a deep, sustained, loving, and also ambivalent, bond. They are friends who would appear to have had some prior romantic possibility (they were briefly engaged in college, but Midge broke it off), the melancholy fumes of which still hang in the air. Their genuine, funny rapport is suffused with warmth and wit, yet they are curiously adrift and isolated even with each other (figs. 4 and 5).

For both Scottie and Midge, sexuality appears to be inextricable from isolation. They are not involved in a romantic or sexual relationship with each other, but they are also not

Figure 6. "A do-it-yourself type of thing."

involved in sexual or romantic relationships with anyone else. The importance of this aspect of their characterizations lies in one of the overarching concerns of Hitchcock's films from the late-1950s to the mid-1960s: in the modern era, sexuality has become as constricted, if not thwarted altogether, as personal identity. For these reasons, the motif of masturbation in *Vertigo* sheds light on the concerns of *Marnie* as well as this period of Hitchcock's career. My effort to draw out the pathos in solitary sex is not meant to suggest that it is inherently indicative of failure. Indeed, on some level onanistic/masturbatory sexuality might be seen as a dimension of queer resilience in that it suggests an alternative to normative forms of sexuality. Yet, inescapably, solitary sex functions as a complex sign of failure (of intimacy, of fulfillment) in the films I am discussing.

I detect two possible coded references to masturbation in Scottie and Midge's conversation: first, when Scottie is discussing the removal of his corset he announces that he'll be able to scratch himself like everybody else; second, in the exchange about the bra and the aircraft engineer down the peninsula who designed it (fig. 6):

SCOTTIE: How's your love life, Midge?
MIDGE: There's following a train of thought!
SCOTTIE: Well? . . .
MIDGE: Normal.

I think on first hearing that the "train of thought" here seems to be about the bra (which, remember, Scottie doesn't recognize as such: "What's this doohickey?"). This scene is structured partly around two pieces of women's underclothing, one worn by a man, the other worn by no one. The bra, as object, symbolizes a woman's attractiveness to men, especially when it works like a cantilever bridge and leaves no straps visible, preserving the workings of the feminine mystique for the male gaze. Naturally, it also suggests Midge's love life to Scottie, even though for her it is simply an object she is being paid to draw. I think, however, the more immediate connection to the "do-it-yourself type thing" should also be understood as part of the train of thought here. Beneath the radar of the Hollywood censors, this scene may subtly imply that both Scottie and Midge serve as their own instruments of sexual gratification.[11]

Vertigo will transform the more playful suggestions of this early scene into the grimmest portrait of male-female relationships in Hitchcock (until *Frenzy*). The theme of modernity, sexuality, the urban, and entrapment—the private traps—will, eventually, narrow down to a lonely, isolated woman's negotiation of the vast, barren, and exhaustingly demanding social world in *Marnie*, with masturbation here once again emerging as one of the most viable forms of sexual expression—perhaps the only one that is a personal expression—in such an environment.

What I want to suggest is that masturbation emerges as the alternative to sexual relationships with other people when we remember that it is possible to experience such relationships as compulsory, alien, a social demand, not something one necessarily wishes to pursue. Indeed, onanistic themes inform many Hitchcock films—one thinks of L.B. Jefferies (Stewart again) scratching an itch in *Rear Window* (1954) and then audibly sighing in relief afterwards, of Norman Bates's peep-show-like viewing of Marion Crane in *Psycho*—and emerges in *Marnie* as an alternative form of sexuality that resists the typings and terminologies of the sexualizing social order. Marnie's life is a do-it-yourself kind of thing.[12] The thematic of onanism is precisely what makes the attempted robbery of Mark's own safe so erotically charged—a scene between Marnie and a metal, heavy *thing*, rather than another person. Hitchcock films this moment as a feverish, illicit sexual encounter. Her sly, knowing, anticipatory looks at and handling of the safe, and kinky, fetishistic gloved hands, all convey the erotic nature of the depiction. What is significant about the scene is that it eroticizes Marnie's relationship with a non-living thing. The thematic of onanistic sexuality reaches a particular level of intensity in the fox-hunt sequence, a kind of referendum on Marnie's do-it-yourself sexuality as well as the larger issues of class, sexuality, and their intersection.

As I suggested in the discussion of Marnie's apartness, it both corresponds to the theme of unbearable loneliness and represents a compensatory pleasure that allows Marnie to exist in the social. For all of the danger and panic that inhere in her stealing and series of fake identities, her overall fake life, Marnie is, for the most part, surprisingly comfortable in the alternative existence she carves out for herself, and this private pleasure is depicted in an increasingly erotic register. While it would be absurd to champion this life of stealing and lying, to overlook the negative, even pathological aspects of Marnie's behavior and fail to see how indicative it is of her deep despair, the extent to which she seems to enjoy herself—on her own—is significant. The shot of her raising her restored-blonde head from the sink in which her black hair-dye was rinsed out that concludes the opening section of the film, specifically the smile on her face as she does so that is amplified by the "Marnie theme" in Bernard Herrmann's score; the shots of her riding Forio, blonde hair flowing in the breeze, as she smiles rapturously, an effect again enhanced by the triumphalism of Herrmann's scoring here; even the shot of her arriving in Philadelphia, where Rutland's publishing company is located, quietly smiling as she surveys her new surroundings—such moments convey a sense of her possibilities and a kind of pleasurable inhabiting of her own life. (Indeed, it is contact with others, including her mother and the little Jessie, that mess things up for meticulous Marnie.) What I mean by Marnie's onanism is not the actual practice of masturbation—though this may indeed be an aspect of what's being represented—but rather a disposition, potentiality, tone, and sensibility, a series of private pleasures that remain private, again a means of inhabiting without contact. Certainly, in Marnie's case, the contact avoided powerfully includes male-female genital contact.

Marnie's seeming comfort with apartness—*pace* E.M. Forster, "only connect" does not seem to be her motivating philosophy—contrasts sharply with her intensely palpable longing for maternal intimacy. One of the most moving scenes in the film is also one of the briefest: Marnie, in her first day as mistress of Rutland house, calling up her mother to reconnect with her and to reassure her that she is alright, a conversation that scheming Lil overhears and uses to expose Marnie to Mark. Mother remains the only person in Marnie's life to whom she can turn. It is never clear that she would like or even needs intimate bonds beyond those she ardently pursues with her mother. As becomes clear almost immediately, encounters with her mother, far from being a respite from her masquerade and endangerment, routinely trigger Marnie's anger and sorrow, as indicated by the early scene with the overturned pecans in her mother's kitchen. This scene is emblematic of the impasse and also the potential violence within this chilly yet intimate relationship, a recurring motif being that violence erupts within our closest affiliations. This moment in which Marnie—who is certainly presented as being desperately in need of the talking cure—articulates her sorrow and her frustration to her mother leads to Marnie's angry accusations and to Mrs. Edgar slapping her when the accusations pierce too deeply. Marnie does speak here, eloquently asking, "Why don't you love me, Mama? I've always wondered why you don't. You never give me one part of the love you give Jessie."

She also asks her mother why she always pulls away from her: when Marnie puts her hand on her mother's, Mrs. Edgar withdraws her hand as if it's been bitten by a snake. The mother-daughter relationship is the basis of all social interactions in the film, including those that are sexually charged, the template for the tender-terrible relationship between Marnie and Mark and for the attraction/repulsion relationship between Marnie and Lil. The antithetical poles of desire as established within the film are the onanistic and the properly heterosexual. Queer/gay/lesbian forms of desire emerge within a larger continuum of desire in the film.

Despite Marnie's palpable feelings of loss—I can think of no major character in a Hitchcock film who is as deeply bereft, perhaps not even Norman Bates; though this is not a point I would make emphatically, he can possess the mother in his own mind at least, even if this possession clearly brings him grief and inspires his murderous violence—one almost gets the sense that, and this is merely to echo the heroine herself, Marnie would be content were she and her mother the only people in the world. The mother who will not give the gift of love is still the mother one has, the *only* mother one has. The theme of *compensatory consolation* emerges in the considerable pleasure Marnie derives from buying and presenting her mother with expensive gifts and from having them received and enjoyed by her, at least to a limited extent. Palpably conflicted as she receives them, smiling but also admonishing her daughter for spending so much, Mrs. Edgar seems to have a sixth sense that these gifts have been illicitly procured. Money serves as both conduit to and barrier against love and affection, in every sense the economy of desire in this film, as it is in the first half of *Psycho*.[13]

"Are You Still in the Mood for Killing?": *Class, Aesthetics, and the Fox-Hunting Sequence*

The recent turn in queer theory to questions of class helpfully enlarges our understanding of *Marnie's* exploration of similar questions. The definitive reading of *Marnie* as a film about the trauma of class differences is Michele Piso's essay "Mark's Marnie." As she eloquently argues, in *Marnie* "the world of capital dominates and chills the erotic and creative aspects of life."[14] Piso focuses our attention on the discarded, abandoned Mrs. Edgar at the end of the film, and interprets the expressionistic trope of the red suffusions of color as a symbolic rendering of the "blood of the terrified and violated body, the blood of women, of murder and rape...the red of suffering."[15] Lucretia Knapp reads "the blood that washes over Marnie's eyes" as maternal blood, "horrifically fetishized."[16] The scarlet suffusions of the film link it to another supreme American text about mothers, daughters, the criminal woman, and morally suspect masculinity, Nathaniel Hawthorne's *The Scarlet Letter* (1850). Marnie's mother's sexual trauma as well as Marnie's own—the violation of both—deepens the resonances of the fox-hunt scene, as I will show. This sequence brilliantly foregrounds the traumas of class and female sexuality and critiques them on a formal level.

What is particularly interesting about *Marnie* in cinematic terms is the extent to which Hitchcock's depiction of—and, I would argue, investment in—the heroine's estrangement dovetails with an experimental and daring series of anti-realistic and meta-cinematic motifs, flourishes, and sequences. For example, the bathroom stall scene in which Marnie hides out as the workers depart evokes film noir through its use of chiaroscuro; at the end of the street in the run-down neighborhood in Baltimore in which Mrs. Edgar lives looms a jarringly artificial matted-in ship, calling attention to the film's constructed nature and, more generally, to film's relationship to the other arts, such as painting. Similarly, anti-realistic and meta-cinematic elements inform the fox-hunt-sequence (fig. 7). Its rigorous formal beauty makes the sequence, harrowing though it is, exhilarating. The vigor of art is a force that transcends the despair and the abjection so exquisitely thematized here. A kinship exists in the film between the ways in which Marnie can use her trauma as a means of negotiating her social abjection and the ways in which Hitchcock's poetic aestheticization allows him to find beauty in the unremitting narrative bleakness of this work. The mixture of "natural" and realistic footage and

Figure 7. Marnie at the hunt.

studio-bound, "anti-realistic" techniques aesthetically mirror the tensions in the heroine's own psychology, between her experience of the "real" world and her fabricated alternative private world.

The fox-hunt sequence is a bravura reinterpretation of the rabbit-and-bird-hunting scene in Jean Renoir's *The Rules of the Game* (1939), another film about the strictures of class and desire. In the fox-hunt and its aftermath, *Marnie* depicts society as a life-in-death ritual, in which cruel merriment animates the social actors and gives the performance of social relations their vitality. Clad in their posh hunting clothes, which blur the lines of gender difference and make everyone look "mannish," the aristocrats on their horses, along with the aptly named hounds they have trained, chase a lone fox to its death. The uniformity of their appearances makes the riders/hunters seem like a procession of clones. At the same time, the fox hunt is depicted as absurdly grandiose, phalanxes of predators in pursuit of so lowly a prey. Hitchcock offers a microcosmic social satire (made more deeply resonant still by what it implies about the English Hitchcock's late re-encounter with one of his own culture's most famous social rituals, albeit here transplanted to an American setting). He also offers a deadly serious political allegory for the heroine's relationship to Mark Rutland's entire moneyed world, over which, as his wife, she is presumed to be able to comfortably preside.

Hitchcock's use of rear-projection—initially seen as indicative of his carelessness, failing powers, datedness, or lack of inspiration, even by critics as perceptive and supportive as the auteurist Andrew Sarris, an early Hitchcock champion—is an exquisitely apposite means of rendering the fox-hunting aristocrats' simultaneous motion and encasement in nullity.[17] In process shots against a rear-projected background, the riders in profile bob up and down on their horses. They twitch with life while being utterly disconnected from life—vitality, true movement—a stasis conveyed by the artificiality of the cinematic techniques Hitchcock employs. Marnie is shown to be one of the riders, encased in life-in-deathness; the crucial maneuver will be to jolt her out of this stasis and into movement, even as this seeming movement is depicted as itself a form of stylized, artificially constructed movement. Hitchcock has often been discussed in the context of Edgar Allan Poe, whom he frequently cited as an important influence. The linkages between both artists come to near-explicit fruition in *Marnie*, in the Baltimore (where Poe died and is buried) setting of Mrs. *Edgar*, also called Miss *Bernice* by Jessie, evoking Poe's title character *Berenice* (even Marnie evokes the names of Poe women such as Morella, Annabel Lee, Ligeia, in its unusual and single-word-all-encompassing qualities). Of particular importance in Poe as an intertext for Hitchcock is his thematization of life-in-deathness. For example, in Poe's one novel, *The Narrative of Arthur Gordon Pym* (1838), shipwrecked sailors discover to their horror that the figure who appears to be waving at them happily, promising rescue, is actually a rotting corpse given the uncanny semblance of life by the carrion bird pecking away at his body. Hitchcock extends Poe's effects of life-in-death to a stringent class critique. The social order in *Marnie* is always already deadening and dead, but the violent urges and persistent fantasies of its actors give it an uncanny, death-in-life vitality, as the cartoonish shots of the riders bobbing up and down suggests. Rear projection as Hitchcock deploys it (in Marnie's first ride on Forio and in the fox-hunt) functions as an allegory of entrapment that overrides fantasies of escape and movement; rear projection reifies stasis as the mode of existence.

Paradoxically, however, it is Marnie's very trauma that gives her some semblance of actual feeling and freedom.

Figure 8. Cruel merriment.

Figure 9. Marnie's critical gaze.

Distressed as she looks upon the fox being torn to bits by the dogs as the callous aristocrats chortle at the mayhem, Marnie scans her fellow riders in horror (see figs. 8 and 9). Suddenly, she sees one rider in a red jacket, a blinding blaze of her traumatically charged color. As one of the expressionistic red suffusions that signal Marnie's "seizures," as Knapp puts it, engulfs the screen, an effect heightened by Bernard Herrmann's dramatic musical motif for the effect, Marnie suddenly has the energy to escape the scene of carnage, class warfare, and exhibitionistic cruelty.[18] The sight of the color red provokes her painful, maddening seizure, but it also provides the jolt of recognition that frees her from her social and cultural imprisonment within the hunt, depicted as a ritualistic bloodletting on literal and symbolic levels. Her seizure allows her to take immediate, furious flight on her horse from this scene of savagery. I believe that this scene embodies the major subject of Hitchcock's film. Trauma, isolation, and loneliness, horrific though they are, are also defining elements of the social outcast's resourcefulness. As I have elaborated, queer resilience is an ambiguous and ambivalent concept, one with positive and negative manifestations. Here, Marnie's resilience emerges from her empathetic connection to the violated animal. Like the fox, Marnie is pursued and hunted by the demands of the social order; and if the fox-hunt is class ritual par excellence, valences exist between it and Marnie's violations. The tea service scene, while no blood is shed during it, is in its own way another kind of hunt—a rooting out of class undesirables.

I would add that what Marnie may be experiencing here is shame. Shame has direct relevance to queer experience. Drawing on the work of Silvan Tompkins, Eve Kosofsky Sedgwick writes:

> One of the strange features of shame, but perhaps also the one that offers the most conceptual leverage for political projects, is the way bad treatment of someone else, bad treatment *by* someone else, someone else's embarrassment, stigma, debility, bad smell, or strange behavior, seemingly having nothing to do with me, can so readily flood me—assuming I'm a shame-prone person—with this sensation whose very suffusiveness seems to delineate my precise, individual outlines in the most isolating way possible.[19]

Marnie feels ashamed of the social class of which she is now a member—their grotesque display of indifference to and mockery of suffering—while also feeling tremendous levels of shame herself. The hard outlines of individual identity melt away in the "suffusive" flood of empathetic shame. Marnie's connection to her own constitutive, core pain allows her to feel for the violated animal and to escape from the collective banalization of cruelty and violence, if only for a moment. If shame is part of queer resilience, we can understand the positive and negative affect that mutually define the concept. The shame Marnie feels comes very close to ruining, even to extinguishing (as in the suicide attempt after sex with Mark), her life; this shame is also precisely what allows her to escape a scene of psychological and physical torment and also finally to articulate a moral sensibility: as she later challenges Lil, "Are you still in the mood for killing?"

George Tomasini's editing and Robert Burks's austere, autumnal cinematography contribute vitally to the meanings made manifest here. The editing creates a sexual momentousness, a movement from premonitory anticipations of release to the final climactic devastation of Forio's crash against the second embankment. The scattershot editing of the bodies—Marnie's and the horse's—falling on the ground further conveys the sense that this would-be orgasmic release has become a confusion of pain and panic. Marnie's control of the situation sputters, along with the images, wildly, incoherently out of control. But at the same time, Burks's austere colors convey an overall sense of somber detachment from the proceedings, of nature as itself a life-in-death. It is in this stringent rendering of the scene-in-nature that the sequence's expressionistic dimensions come through most forcefully.

Adding an ambiance of perversity, Marnie's horse can be read as a tipping of the hat to Buñuel, the great Surrealist whom Hitchcock admired, and his frequent and almost always perverse horse and animal imagery. The film explores the varieties of sexual possibility, ranging from lesbian desire (Lil and Marnie, Marnie and her mother) to fetishism (Marnie's purse, her gloved hands) to lesbian fetishism (the fur coat that Marnie gives Mrs. Edgar, who seems visibly pleased by it, evoking the shot of the most clearly lesbian character in the Hitchcock canon, Mrs. Danvers [Judith Anderson] holding up Rebecca's lustrous fur to the second Mrs. de Winter's trembling face) to bestiality to onanism. One could argue that Hitchcock explores the emotional undercurrents beneath sexual perversity, the motivations and the sheer need behind Marnie's relationship to her horse, no mere gallant steed here but the stand-in for sexuality itself. The montage effect of rapidly shifting views of Marnie riding and of what she sees before her (landscape; then embankments to be leaped over, the first one successfully, the second one a fatal disaster for Forio), accentuated by a gathering aural momentum—the diegetic one of the horse's furiously pounding hooves, the non-diegetic one of Herrmann's hammeringly intense score, building in this passage to a climax all its own—contributes greatly to the sequence's metaphorical meanings and value as an allegory of sexual intercourse.

Marnie is a film about the varieties of sexual experience, but it focuses on two modes of sex specifically: first the sex-as-rape theme associated with Mark's violation of Marnie on the ship and also the traumatic backstory of the film involving Marnie, her mother, and the sailor; second, the masturbatory sexuality associated with Marnie and her horse rides, suggesting the idea that it is only with Forio that she can experience true, and possibly sexual, liberation. As a sexual symbol, Forio is most obviously a substitute phallus or a phallic prop. Given Marnie's animosity toward the idea of male sexuality, I argue that Forio functions as a metaphor for—and, perhaps, also a means of achieving—self-pleasure rather than intercourse with another person (including another woman), on every level of that term. The montage of Marnie riding bears the burden of thematizing both sex-as-rape and Marnie's onanistic sexuality, figured here as both wildly out of control and also a wounded compensation for the social abnegation she suffers within her marriage to the wealthy Mark, a class malaise further allegorized by the class-based savagery of the hunt.

Revisiting the Primal Scene

Though it delves into frequent indications that sexuality is a complex and wide-ranging category of human experience, the film centrally frames sex in terms of Mark's question "Sex?" in the free-association game, the question about what to do about, how to achieve, how to resolve, how to acquire heterosexual sexual legitimacy. All of the film's attendant questions regarding self, solitude, authenticity, relationships, the moral, even the animal, depend on this central question. I want to turn now to the question of rape that has loomed, and continues to do so, over the film since its initial production.

Mark Rutland, as played by the 1960s sex symbol Sean Connery, who famously first played James Bond and has been seen as the epitome of hairy-chested hunkiness ever since, is a difficult character to make sense of, and it is his sheer incommensurability as a character that provides a basis for thinking of him not merely as a patriarchal, moneyed, masculinist brute and rapist—and I believe that we cannot shy away from this word—but as a flawed and suffering human character worthy, like Marnie, Mrs. Edgar, and others, of sympathy precisely for these reasons. Mark wields white male heterosexual privilege with terrific zeal, almost salivating as he boasts, to Marnie herself, about having trapped and "caught" her. His entire plan to blackmail her into marriage is as barbaric and cruel as it is woefully misguided. Yet he is also a bewildered and in some ways poignant male character who adopts, identifies with, the female subject position. His question "Sex" is not articulated, as Connery compellingly plays him, as a determined and knowing one. Instead, Mark's affect as he raises the question is shy, almost abashed, uttered as if from a position of an essential bewilderment.

Nevertheless, I believe that Robin Wood missteps in exculpating Mark to the extent that he does in his revised analysis of *Marnie*. Raising the question, "Does Mark save Marnie?" Wood replies that yes, he does—but more important, she saves herself.[20] Alas, I do not find much salvation at the end of *Marnie*, though its surface text does appear to follow the therapeutic-cure model of films like Hitchcock's *Spellbound* (1945) (which I would argue, like *Marnie*, disrupts the model) and *The Three Faces of Eve* (1957). If Marnie gains a "local" knowledge about her own backstory, she is nevertheless fixed within the general bind of the social order and its resolute commitment to the heterosexualization of all of its subjects.

Tapping on the wall to trigger Marnie's memories of her childhood trauma, Mark inhabits both the role of the sailors who tapped on the door of the prostitute mother's window to be let in to her apartment and Marnie's unconscious life. He joins in with it, extending and sharing in it. But he is also, like Verena Tarrant's exploitative huckster father in Henry James's novel *The Bostonians* (1886), the male who "starts" the woman so that she can speak, in Verena's case the stirring language of feminist reform that flows out, ventriloquistically, from her android-like body, in Marnie's case the "truth" of the sexual case history. While the therapeutic model that Wood steadfastly adheres to insists on this truth as a liberating one, it is also clear that for the film and its heroine, it is a revealed truth that only leads to further imprisonment—perhaps the deepest one of all: Marnie's willing submission to social conformity, signified in her submission to the law ("I want to clear it all up") and to marriage to Mark ("I don't want to go to jail, Mark—I'd rather stay with you").

To recall Piso's analysis, red in the film is the color of female victimization. That the scene of violence, both physical and sexual, in the sailor-death-flashback, provides the explanatory basis for Marnie's seizures and general traumatization more than confirms Piso's reading. Marnie is specifically cast as the witness to the scene of adult sexual relations, evoking Freud's theory of the primal scene. The sequence brilliantly opens with a fisheye-lens view of Mrs. Edgar taking Marnie out of the bedroom and putting her to sleep on the sofa, where she will sleep while Mrs. Edgar has sex with the sailor (Bruce Dern), who pays for this service. Hitchcock's use of the fisheye-lens and its odd effects, such as foreshortening the bodily forms of the actors, emphasizes the act of looking and the entire flashback as a scene of voyeuristic looking and/or witnessing. In effect, we the viewers return to the primal scene along with Marnie. The original definition of the primal scene, as Freud elaborates it in *From the History of an Infantile Neurosis*, more commonly known as "The Wolf-Man," involved a vision, imagined or literal, of one's parents having sex with each other.[21] What the child Marnie witnessed and recalls is not, strictly or technically speaking, a primal scene, but instead functions as a kind of collage of elements from Freud's theory of the same. Part of what makes the film's climax shocking is the primal scene elements of the mother's sexuality on display. More important, in evoking the primal scene, the film serves as an archetype of male-female sexual relations, and here the archetype is shot through with violence, violation, and suffering.

Critics have debated whether or not the sailor is endangering—i.e., molesting, or about to molest—the child Marnie. I believe that there is evidence to support the view that he may indeed be violating her. There is an unmistakable shot of the sailor burying his face into the little girl's neck, which to my mind exceeds the desire merely to comfort the girl. In any event, the key point is that Marnie is upset by his ministrations, even if what this signifies is that she is upset by the fact that he, not her mother, is there. And it is her discomfort that provokes Mrs. Edgar's wildly protective wrath. In the chaotic, confused violence that ensues, the sailor falls on Mrs. Edgar, specifically on her "leg," causing her injury. Amid the flailing bodies, her mother's shrieks, and also the sailor's cries, the child Marnie is also screaming.

What is not being represented here on a literal level is the act of heterosexual sex. I argue, however, that, in its disorganized slew of images and sounds of pain, and, specifically, in the extremely graphic shot of the sailor's hairy legs entwined with the mother's legs, the act of heterosexual sex—to the fullest extent possible for a mainstream narrative film of the 1960s—is precisely what is being depicted here, as a seething, sorrowful vision of violation and violence in which the child is traumatized by what she hears as well as sees. In killing the sailor, Marnie is simultaneously protecting her mother and destroying her own innocence. Moreover, the child becomes the mother, the mother the child: Mrs. Edgar, initially protecting her daughter, begs the little Marnie for help. And Marnie responds, battering the sailor with an iron poker. In a wildly horrific effect, Hitchcock focuses on the spreading splotch of red blood on the sailor's white shirt. Sexuality itself becomes the chaotic scene of violence that will then inform all of Marnie's experience of the social order. Sexual violence lies at the heart of the social order, rendering all of its prettifying, hollow, chimerical masquerades deeply suspect and deeply alienating—or, at the very least, so *Marnie* suggests.

In my view, *Marnie* is, ultimately, Hitchcock's most direct and emphatic statement on the maddening and menacing effects of the heterosexism of our culture. Hitchcock's work includes images of loving, tender encounters and possibilities between men and women. But it is also definitively full of images of the terror and violence that inhere in the social order and within individual lives as a result of the insistent heterosexualization of all subjects. Various forms of resistance, many criminal, all illusory—but somehow no less heroic and moving for being that—to this institutionalized sexual normativity are explored in *Marnie*. I have attempted to evoke these forms of resistance throughout the essay— onanistic, lesbian, fetishistic, and queer forms of sexuality threaten to topple the reign of phallic monism. But let me add—and this allows me to turn, at last, to the shipboard rape scene—that the most daring element in the film's deconstruction of the heterosexism inherent in the social order is that it extends its critique to an analysis of the ways in which heterosexual male desire is also distorted and disfigured through this system.

Marnie's Mark

One of the most perplexing trends in criticism of *Marnie*, and from extremely thoughtful critics at that, is the tendency to find, through ever-more strenuous means, a way to exculpate Mark Rutland from charges of rape in the shipboard scene in which he forces Marnie, now his wife, to submit to him sexually. Deborah Thomas rightly argues that, on the one hand, it is unfair and insupportable to think of Mark as a completely negative character and, on the other hand, that the film becomes far richer if we are alert to ways in which Marnie's problems play out across numerous characters in the film, including Mark, whose own family history is problematic and worthy of our sympathy. Nevertheless, I believe that a disquieting critical trend to read the ship-scene as indicative of just about anything other than rape needs to be addressed. To fail to see this scene as an act of supreme violation is to miss out on precisely why Hitchcock fought to keep it in the film. And a proper understanding of Mark as a sympathetic as well as morally dubious character need not be jettisoned in order to understand the scene's meanings—indeed, it is essential to understanding them. The ship-scene is a set-piece study in intimate violence and violation. It is the ultimate love-scene-filmed-as-a-murder-scene in the Hitchcock canon.

William Rothman takes great pains to free Mark from charges of rape.[22] Undergirding this view would appear to be the assumption that somehow Mark does not "know" he is raping Marnie. During the Hitchcock Centennial Conference held at NYU in 1999, questions over this scene and the question of rape were frequently posed to the screenwriter, Jay Presson Allen, by commentators such as Robin Wood and Slavoj Žižek. She was hired to replace the previous screenwriter, Evan Hunter (who had written the screenplay for *The Birds*, and quit working with Hitchcock during the filming of *Marnie* precisely because of his protest over this controversial scene). One exchange, between Presson and Robin Wood, is particularly relevant and has been once again discussed by Tania Modleski in a recent essay. When asked about this scene, Allen concurred with Wood's assessment that while Marnie knows that she is being raped, Mark does not know that he is raping Marnie.[23]

ROBIN WOOD: Can I also, at risk of pushing this too much, go back to the so-called rape scene once more? I've always been bothered by the simple description of that as a rape. I think it's more ambiguous, the way Hitchcock shoots it and perhaps the way you wrote it. . . . Now, the

way I read it, Marnie knows that she is being raped but
Mark does not know he is raping her.
JAY PRESSON ALLEN: You're absolutely right. (20)

Earlier in the discussion Allen noted that she found Evan
Hunter's objections to the scene "psychologically a little
naïve," and further explained that "There's a vast audience of
women out there who fantasize about the idea of rape, as has
been proved over and over and over again" (5). Later, she
cited *Gone with the Wind* (1939) as an example of a film that
contains a rape that no one ever complains about: "Clark
Gable raped Scarlett. I've never heard anybody complain
about that" (10). One of the audience members, Susan White,
made the point that, "Scarlett liked the rape and Marnie
didn't," which, to my mind, sums up just about every
difference between the films' approaches to female sexuality.
(This is not, to be clear, a negative judgment on *Gone with the
Wind*, which is a film I greatly admire. But that film is about
the famished intensity of its heroine's desire, while *Marnie* is
about the attempt to defer desire.)

As Allen's own responses suggest, longstanding
controversies exist about what constitutes rape. While I
personally find Allen's comments about women's rape
fantasies bewildering in this context—the specific context of
Marnie and its meanings—they indicate the difficulties of
sorting out the sexual politics of the era in which the film was
made and released, which held views about marital rape
distinct from those generally held today. In saying "we," of
course, I am on slippery ground. In August of 2012, Missouri
Representative Todd Aiken, defending his anti-abortion
stance, offered theories about "legitimate rape" in which he
claimed that women's bodies instinctively and automatically
defend themselves against pregnancy in cases of "real" rape.
These ill-informed opinions were immediately controversial,
but that they could still be put forth by an educated American
in the year 2012 gives one altogether too vivid an
understanding of just how longstanding the nauseating view
of rape as a debatable phenomenon has been. While historical

work on legal and social views definitions of marital sexuality and marital rape in the 1960s would no doubt enlarge the understanding we have about *Marnie*, I believe that the text itself, closely analyzed, tells us what we need to know about the film's own stance regarding the scene, which reverberates in all of the action that narratively follows, up until the very last shot of the film.

Hitchcock makes it clear that Mark knows full well he is not only violating Marnie, but raping her. The first definition of rape in the *Oxford English Dictionary* is:

> **Noun:** the crime, typically committed by a man, of forcing another person to have sexual intercourse with the offender against their will.[24]

I see no way in which to read the scene other than as a representation of this act so defined. In my view, if we do not understand Mark's psychological awareness, and that of the filmmaker as well, we fail to understand everything that the film stands for and everything it has to offer us as a critique of gendered and sexual roles and relations in capitalism. Indeed, Mark's blackmailing of Marnie into marriage could be taken as a symbolic form of rape, harkening to ancient times:

> *literary:* the abduction of a woman, especially for the purpose of having sexual intercourse with her: *the Rape of the Sabine Women. (OED)*

In many ways, Mark abducts this woman, cutting her off from all she knows. Certainly he imprisons her, installing himself as jailer, warden, counselor, and sexually starved cellmate.

In raping Marnie, Mark is betraying his own principles. To clarify: Mark is proceeding from the basis of his physical and emotional desires to possess Marnie sexually, even though he knows full well—intellectually and also, given his Hitchcock-like ambivalent identification with the suffering woman, emotionally as well—that she will experience sexual intercourse with him as an unbearable violation. It is precisely because he continues to force her to submit to him sexually despite his intimate knowledge of her revulsion toward the sexual act and his genuine feelings of tenderness toward her, tender feelings he expresses physically in the moment in which he places his own robe around her naked body that the scene is so devastatingly angering, sad, powerful—and absolutely crucial not only to the film but to Hitchcock's body of work.

What precedes the sequence in which Mark forces Marnie to submit to him are, first, the scene in which Marnie, almost literally a cornered animal defensively snarling at Mark, angrily and also pitiably demands Mark never to "touch her" ("I cannot stand to be handled," making the hand-as-violation theme nearly explicit), and, second, the montage, of sorts, of different views of the couple in different locations of the ship at different times, wearing different outfits, in each location and having different kinds of conversations. These conversations range from an almost clinical one about the life they will lead together ("I assumed I would be a society wife?") to the often-discussed one in which Mark's anthropological and zoological fascinations now take the form of a monologue about a Kenyan flower that is actually composed of hundreds of insects. The different views of the couple signify visually what is the central preoccupation of the film: sexual difference. We are given, or taken on, a brief tour of the varieties of male-female interaction—standing at the prow of the ship (casual), having an elegant meal for which they are elegantly attired (formal)—all of which are, in effect, a put-on, however many real feelings bubble beneath the charade. These scenes are the beginnings of a lengthy deconstruction of marriage as the ultimate form of social theater, in which men and women perform their respective marital roles. This will become explicit, as the scene on the couple's first morning back from their honeymoon evinces. As Marnie walks Mark to the door (and even here she seems to be led), Mark, with an ironic tone that does not undercut the political pointedness of the exchange, instructs Marnie about how to behave as a proper wife, including giving her husband a public peck on the cheek as he departs. This scene ends with Marnie telling Mark that she doesn't have any money, reinforcing her child-like helplessness and the political understanding of marriage as a social institution in which the wife depends on the husband for subsistence. *Marnie* is the fulfillment of Hitchcock's films of this period in which, as I suggested earlier, the figure of the "wife" is submitted to consistent analysis, clearly a theme with relevance to the Cold War-era redomestication of femininity.

The scene of marital rape commences with a discussion, laced with irony and anger, that begins, as momentous discussions frequently do, with a quotidian dilemma: Marnie asking Mark if he would mind if she shuts the door to the bedroom because the light in the sitting-room, where Mark is reading a book called *Animals of the Seashore*, bothers her. In a facetious tone, Mark responds that we couldn't possibly have anything bothering Marnie, now, could we? Marnie, not missing out on his sarcasm, counters with another question: "How long?" To her elaboration of the question, which refers to how long their dreadful honeymoon on the ship will last, he responds with continued facetiousness, why would anyone want these "halcyon" days to end? Interestingly, this scene comes right after the dinner conversation about the Kenyan flower, implying that he was attempting to stimulate her interest in him as well as the botanical subject. Marnie slams the door, and it is at this point that Mark throws his book down angrily, gets up, opens the door to the bedroom, and confronts Marnie. In response, she adamantly tells him that she wants to go to bed. "I *also* want to go to bed, Marnie," and his sexual meaning becomes clear, because it is at this point that Marnie looks deeply alarmed and cries out—as, we will learn, she did as a child seeing her mother being hurt by the sailor—"*No!*" Mark yanks off her robe and she stands naked before him. There is a pause, and then he approaches her.

The intimate violence that the film has explored—including the moment where Mrs. Edgar slaps Marnie during their fight, even the ways in which Marnie betrays the trust not only of her employers but also of her trusting, potential friend Susan Clabon—comes to the fore here. After Mark has denuded Marnie, he then, with exquisite gentleness, puts his own robe around her shoulders. (One thinks of the line in *Paradise Lost* that Milton uses to describe the shame of the newly fallen, naked Adam as he dons clothing for the first time: "he covered, but his robe / Uncovered more [IX.1058-59].) I believe that the apologetic, and moving, tenderness of this gesture has led some critics to believe that rape is not what is going on here, but it is not the full story of the scene, and, again, it is a key facet of the film's subject. It is precisely the people we love the most (Mrs. Edgar) and people who love us the most (Mark; the undemonstrative, secretly loving Mrs. Edgar) who can be our keenest violators. The tenderness that Mark expresses, in the end, may have much more to do with his own desires—his tender regard for his own tender regard for Marnie, if you will—than with his desire to "bring Marnie out" sexually, to show her that she can experience genital contact in a loving fashion and find it pleasurable, emotionally satisfying, hopefully both.

There is an extraordinary over-the-shoulder (Mark's shoulder) shot of Marnie as Mark, with a magical, uncanny gliding effect that recalls Miriam Haines's slow, steady descent into the grass as Bruno Anthony murders her in *Strangers on a Train* (1951), forces her down to the bed. Marnie's expression—as conveyed through Tippi Hedren's remarkably nuanced, varied, resonant performance, alive to every contour of Marnie's emotional life—is fixed, blank, inert (fig. 10).[25] Disassociation has been linked to childhood sexual abuse and other traumatic experiences. Marnie's blank, frozen look conveys life-in-deathness, a floating away of her consciousness as she submits to Mark's power. Her face is an expressionless mask; her blankess conveys deep levels of silent screaming and her disassociative state. (This dissociation will be formally expressed again in the detached, high angle shots of a zombie-like Marnie making her way to

Figure 10. Marnie's frozen blankness.

Mark's safe after she shoots Forio; the theme of life-in-death the ultimate dissociative state] again emerges here, as the inspection of the dead, lifeless safe activates Marnie's coolly erotic desires.)

Perhaps even more fascinating, however, is the close-up that we get of Mark's face. Now, as we see him from Marnie's point of view, his face looks expressionistically stylized, darkly lit, brooding, with a strangely sly, decisive near-grin on his face that almost, almost recalls Norman Bates's death-head's grin at the end of *Psycho*. One also remembers the introduction to Cary Grant's character Devlin in *Notorious* (1946), shown to us from the back, a seated dark faceless figure, and later shown to us from a funhouse distorted angle as he brings the sleeping Alicia Huberman (Ingrid Bergman) a reviving drink. Hitchcock's dark distortion of heterosexual screen masculinity reaches its apotheosis in *Marnie*, as Mark takes on a carnal and menacing but also uncanny and eerie air as a satanic seducer and ravisher of women. I would offer that, in this film obsessed with the infinite variety of feminine appearances and styles, masculinity, in a remarkably compressed fashion, undergoes a series of shifts and assumes a variety of styles. Mark goes from intellectual husband calmly reading (seemingly calm), to angry husband bursting in on his wife, to sexually demanding husband who will have his way with his wife, to

Figure 11. Mark's Gothic masculinity.

tender, kindly man protecting woman, to rapacious, animalistic male, the gothic image of overpoweringly physical masculinity (fig. 11).

Perhaps the most telling moment in the entire sequence, a *tour de force* of pure cinema, is the one in which Hitchcock's camera puts us in Marnie's subject position, not only emotionally but physically. When Mark says "I also want to go to bed, Marnie," the camera, which had previously held a two-shot image of Mark standing on the left, Marnie on the right (an exquisite visual representation of the emotional impasse between them, rendered in spatial terms) now swings around so that we are facing Mark—so that *we* are now Marnie, facing Mark.

The canted, low angle—an unusual touch—from which we look up as Mark kisses Marnie recalls the scene in Mark's office during the thunderstorm when he first kissed her. There, the perspective of the low, canted angle makes the kiss between man and woman seem alien and uncanny—we should not be seeing lovers passionately kissing from this angle. A scene that foregrounds ancient civilizations (the pre-Columbian art of Mark's dead wife) and the zoological now renders the erotic contact between man and woman as an almost clinical study of the mating ritual. We see Mark's lips drag over the inert expanse of Marnie's face, and even glimpse the adhesive effect of lips on lips, and see lips pull away from lips as well. If we compare this scene to the famous scene of Cary Grant and Ingrid Bergman kissing for an endless duration in long take in *Notorious*—itself a film that deconstructs the couple by dramatizing numerous moments of the violence of intimacy—we can see a remarkable difference in tone. The scene in *Notorious* borders on perversity, but it is unmistakably erotic and powerful for being so ardently expressed in this register; in *Marnie*, however, the kissing scenes convey the awkwardness and the strangeness of the mismatched pairing, however much palpable yearning on Mark's part undergirds it.

I would argue that the class critique is at its most implicit and most resonant in the stateroom sequence. Mark, because of his wealth and his sportsmanship (he is reading *Animals of the Seashore*—clearly, animals are on his mind), feels that he can trap Marnie as if she were an animal and triumph with her as he did with the jaguarondi, getting Marnie, too, to "trust" him. His wealth gives him, as *Vertigo* similarly envisions, the "power and the freedom" to overpower and trap Marnie into sexuality and, later in the film, into discourse, as she is forced, and her mother is forced, to speak the truth of their unspeakable violation. That Mark is himself a feeling, flawed, vulnerable, empathetic, in his own way quite brave character only deepens the poignancy and the horror of this narrative.

Paradoxically, Marnie expresses her queer resilience by attempting to drown herself, transforming the symbol of helpless femininity maddened by male cruelty (the suicide of Ophelia by drowning is an archetype of this) into a form of desperate female agency. Her retort once Mark rescues her and asks her why she did not simply throw herself into the ocean—"The point was to kill myself, not feed the damn fish"—conveys that dark wit, a mordant take on the social, is an element of resilience. Mark, while the upholder of patriarchal power, is also its victim. In some ways, he wills himself into Marnie's Lovelace-like rapist, convincing himself that he is only doing so for her benefit. Moreover, his own bruised ego demands reassurance.

What he says jokingly in one scene—"Is this your way of telling me that you do not find me attractive?"—becomes real need and demand expressed through physical and emotional violence in a subsequent scene. What is not willingly given to us we take, sometimes with an unforgivable violence. Hitchcock, in this pivotal sequence— pivotal in *Marnie* and in his entire body of work—conveys with astonishing power the complexities and pathos of how Marnie is endlessly victimized, by the social order and by those who uphold it, such as Mark—perpetrators who are at least in Mark's instance themselves victims of a system that favors some but truly liberates or humanizes no one.

Conclusion

Other than *Vertigo*, *Marnie* is perhaps Hitchcock's most complex film. *Marnie* presents a view of the world, the American world at least, as fundamentally disordered, but for all that no less ferociously devoted to order. Class and sexual normativity here function as systems for enforcing as well as maintaining this need for order. The powerless must helplessly acquiesce to those in power. In turn, those in power may have good intentions but inevitably fall back on that power and its privileges to get what they want, need, demand, desire. Compulsory heterosexuality both imprisons (Marnie) and impels (Mark), fundamentally distorting all relations, including those of the heterosexually oriented. Marnie's Mark—the man who understands Marnie and her violation and life-long vulnerability—struggles forever against money's Mark, the Mark who wields power and crushes those without it, such as Mrs. Edgar, left truly bereft by the end. The question is not, then, does Mark save Marnie, but what can possibly save this culture?

Perhaps the most resonant message in *Marnie* is the idea that, if it does not subsume one, trauma (memory, recurring pain, a feeling of being overpowered or seized by these) can be the foundation for a continued and perhaps even an ethical life. By saying this, I in no way mean to contribute a "positive" reading of Marnie, film or character, that frames both as participating in a redemptive model. But if queer resilience has any resilience at all as a concept, it will be for its ability to illuminate both the positive and the negative aspects of experience, both the dubious and the more heroic aspects of survival in an often unimaginable world.

Notes

1. "Queer Studies and the Crises of Capitalism," *GLQ: A Journal of Lesbian and Gay Studies* 18, no. 1 (2012).

2. See Jean Genet, *Funeral Rites*, trans. Bernard Frechtman (New York: Grove/Atlantic, 1988); Bersani, *Homos* (Cambridge: Harvard University Press, 1995); Edelman, *No Future: Queer Theory and the Death Drive* (Durham: Duke University Press, 2004); and for a counter-response to the queer anti-relation thesis that critiques, in particular, Edelman's disregard for non-white queer aesthetic productions, see José Esteban Muñoz, *Cruising Utopia: The Then and There of Queer Futurity* (New York: NYU Press, 2009). I would add that I have found a great deal of Bersani's work extremely helpful to my own thinking, especially his exploration of Freud's importance as a theorist of sexuality who emphasizes its disturbing aspects.

3. Judith Butler, "Melancholy Gender/Refused Identification," in *The Psychic Life of Power: Theories in Subjection* (Stanford: Stanford University Press, 1997), 132-50, at p. 135.

4. Lucretia Knapp, "The Queer Voice in *Marnie*," in *A Hitchcock Reader*, eds. Marshall Deutelbaum and Leland Poague (Malden, MA: Wiley-Blackwell, 2009), 295-311. See also Raymon Bellour, *The Analysis of Film*, ed. Constance Penley (Bloomington: Indiana University Press, 2000).

5. Knapp, "The Queer Voice in *Marnie*," 302.

6. In my book *Men Beyond Desire: Manhood, Sex, and Violation in American Literature* (New York: Palgrave Macmillan, 2005), I argue that the antebellum period in particular is notable for foregrounding male characters who keep their emotions, bodies, and sexuality severely off-limits, unavailable to other men as well as to women.

7. In this manner, she is the very opposite of the Shirley Maclaine character in William Wyler's flawed but also greatly underrated *The Children's Hour* (1961), the director's second version of Lillian Hellman's play, more explicit about its theme of lesbianism than his first version, *These Three* (1936). The greater explicitness of the lesbian themes of *The Children's Hour* makes this film an important intertext for *Marnie*, a film that has a similar fair-lady/dark-lady physical split, between the desiring schoolteacher Martha Dobie (Maclaine) and the desired schoolteacher Karen Wright (Audrey Hepburn). This split in terms of symbolic female physicalities also informs *The Birds* (1963), of course, in its complex juxtaposition between Tippi Hedren's Melanie Daniels and dark-haired, husky-voiced Suzanne Pleshette's Annie Hayworth. *Marnie* revises the relationship between Maclaine and Hepburn in *The Children's Hour*, making the desired dark lady of that film *the one who desires*, and also making the fair lady—far from someone who wishes to immolate herself because of her desires—sexually unavailable and, for the most part, non-desiring. Maclaine's Martha Dobie in *The Children's Hour* commits suicide by the end of the film because she cannot bear the publically exposed truth of her lesbianism. In *Marnie*, however, sexuality is much closer to an open secret always on the verge of spilling out, as Lil's transgressive sexual asides evince.

8. Marnie's mother is not there in the sense that she is emotionally unavailable. For a fascinating essay on this subject, see Allan Lloyd Smith, "*Marnie*, the Phantom, and the Dead Mother," *Hitchcock Annual* 11 (2002-03): 164-80.

9. William Rothman, "The Universal Hitchcock," in *A Companion to Alfred Hitchcock*, eds. Thomas Leitch and Leland Poague (Malden, MA: Wiley-Blackwell, 2011), 351.

10. In her essay "Self-Posssession and Dispossesson in Hitchcock's *Marnie*," *Hitchcock Annual* 15 (2006-07), 107-122, Deborah Thomas discusses the film's themes of "possession," how everyone and everything in the film can become a possession, and the "linking of personal relationships to material ones" (113). I would argue that the film is about reification, the turning of its human actors into things, and things that belong to the heterosexual social order.

11. My thanks to Alexander J. Beecroft for his insightful comments about this scene.

12. See Eve Kosofsky Sedgwick, "Jane Austen and the Masturbating Girl," in *Tendencies* (Durham: Duke University Press,

1993), 114, for a discussion of masturbation as a socially resistant and sexually unclassifiable erotic mode.

13. The woman's relationship to money is an increasingly important theme in Hitchcock's work from the late 1950s forward. He explores the relationship between woman's sexuality and capital with increasing attentiveness in *To Catch a Thief, Vertigo,* and *North by Northwest,* but it is in his trilogy of femininity of the early 1960s — *Psycho, The Birds,* and *Marnie* — that he truly explores this theme in greater depth, and with *Marnie* especially.

14. Michele Piso, "Mark's Marnie," in *A Hitchcock Reader,* 290.

15. Piso, "Mark's Marnie," 299.

16. Knapp, "The Queer Voice in *Marnie,*" 301.

17. According to Sarris, Hitchcock "miscalculated his effects. The manner is present, but the magic is absent. His fake sets, particularly of dockside Baltimore, have never been more distracting, and the process shots of Tippi on horseback are appallingly dated. Again, the inability of the leads to hold the foreground imposes an extra burden on the background. Who cared if Rio were in process in *Notorious* when Bergman and Grant held the foreground?" See *"Marnie,"* in *Confessions of a Cultist: On the Cinema, 1955-1969* (New York: Simon and Schuster, 1970), 143.

18. Knapp, "The Queer Voice in *Marnie,*" 299.

19. Sedgwick, "Shame, Theatricality, and Queer Performativity: Henry James' *The Art of the Novel,*" *Gay Shame,* ed. David M. Halperin and Valerie Traub (Chicago: Chicago University Press, 2009), 51.

20. Robin Wood, "You Freud, Me Hitchcock," in *Hitchcock's Films Revisited* (New York: Columbia University Press, 2002), 388-406.

21. Sigmund Freud, *From the History of an Infantile Neurosis* (1918). Standard Edition, vol. 17 (London: Hogarth Press, 1955), 7-122.

22. Rothman, "The Universal Hitchcock," 353-54. Rothman is an extremely astute critic of Hitchcock, and this essay brims with resonant readings, but I find the almost languorous evocation of Mark's innocence here unpersuasive.

23. "An Interview with Jay Presson Allen," interviewed by Richard Allen, *Hitchcock Annual* 9 (2000-01), 3-22. Page references for further quotations from this article are cited parenthetically in the main text. For commentary on this interview within the context of a discussion of Hitchcock and feminism, see Tania Modleski, "Suspicion: Collusion and Resistance in the Work of Hitchcock's Female Collaborators," in *A Companion to Alfred Hitchcock,* 177-78. In

this essay Modleski pays close attention to the women who worked with Hitchcock, not just Alma Reville, his wife, but others such as the screenwriter Joan Harrison.

24. http://oxforddictionaries.com/definition/english/rape

25. For an excellent discussion of blankness in *Marnie* and other works, see Susan White, "A Surface Collaboration: Hitchcock and Performance," *A Companion to Alfred Hitchcock*, 181-98.

RICHARD ALLEN

Hitchcock and the Wandering Woman: The Influence of Italian Art Cinema on The Birds

In this paper I will examine how Hitchcock's encounter with Italian art cinema helped to shape his film *The Birds* (1963), and I will pay particular attention to the influence of Michelangelo Antonioni's film *L'Avventura* (*The Adventure*, 1960). In the early 1960s, Hitchcock was highly aware of his status in the eyes of the French critics as a preeminent auteur, since they had been engaging in conversation with him and writing (mostly) laudatory articles ever since he made *To Catch a Thief* (1955).[1] Furthermore, Hitchcock had just made an unprecedented critical and commercial hit in *Psycho* (1960). He was at the apex of both his reputation and success, and yet these came at the very moment that he was challenged and provoked by the remarkable and rapid developments taking place in European art cinema. *The Birds* was conceived by Hitchcock in part as a response to this challenge, a work that would at once continue his commercial success and confirm his status as an auteur on a par with the European directors he so admired. Hitchcock engaged with art cinema to inspire his creativity and sustain his critical reputation.

There is ample evidence that Hitchcock did watch European art cinema, especially Italian films, over a long period of time, and specifically during the making of *The Birds*. His biographer Patrick McGilligan writes that "Hitchcock's love for Italy was genuine; and he kept up with the postwar cinema there."[2] Hitchcock was a particular admirer of De Sica's *Bicycle Thieves* (1948). According to Robert Kapsis, his notebook for the early summer of 1961, as he was preparing to make *The Birds*, records that Hitchcock viewed several European art films: Bergman's *The Virgin Spring* (1960) and *The Magician* (1958), Godard's *Breathless* (1960), and most importantly for my argument, *L'Avventura*.[3] Hitchcock makes an unusually explicit reference to Italian Cinema in *The Birds* when Lydia Brenner (Jessica Tandy) makes disparaging reference to the news stories of Melanie Daniels (Tippi Hedren) cavorting naked in a fountain in Rome. The reference here is very clearly to Anita Ekberg's exploits in the Trevi Fountain in *La Dolce Vita* (Fellini, 1960) but what is evoked here is not simply Fellini's film, but the entire cultural imaginary of Italian movies, Italian sophistication, sexuality, and style at the cusp of the 1960s.[4] After making *The Birds* Hitchcock would record his admiration for Antonioni by exclaiming to Howard Fast, having just seen *Blow-Up* (1966), that "These Italian directors are a century ahead of me in terms of technique!"[5] In the mid-1960s he collaborated with the great Italian script-writing team of Age and Scarpelli (Agenore Incrocci and Furio Scarpelli) on a caper movie set among Italian immigrants in New York called *R.R.R.R.*, though the movie never got off the ground. Also, via Peggy Robertson, he contacted the writer of *Bicycle Thieves*, Cesare Zavattini, to work on the script of what would become *Torn Curtain* (1966), but decided against working on two long-distance collaborations at once.[6]

Hitchcock's attempt to reactivate his career through absorbing the influence of art cinema needs to be understood within the broader context of his early development as a film director and his own subsequent practice. In his twenties, when working as an assistant director for Graham Cutts, Hitchcock had the opportunity to watch the major German directors of the period at work, including Fritz Lang and F.W. Murnau. Hitchcock rightly perceived German directors to be at the cutting edge of story-telling in film, in the way they sought to narrate through "pure cinema" or images alone, and their influence proved decisive on Hitchcock's own approach to narrative technique as well as his treatment of human sexuality on screen. Now in the 1960s, having made a string of films that many have come to regard as his best work, Hitchcock turned once more to developments in European cinema in order to justify his reputation as a great auteur, for he believed that European cinema was again at the cutting edge of film art. It is as if, relatively late in his career, Hitchcock sought to recapture the innovation that inspired the creativity of his youth. It is surely not incidental in this context that *The Birds* was also directly inspired by the story and situation of F.W. Murnau's *Sunrise* (1927), a film that transposes the aesthetic preoccupations of Weimar cinema to Hollywood.[7] In both films, a woman of the city descends upon a village to seduce a man who lives with his family by the water, and both rely on extensive sequences of "pure cinema." In this sense, Hitchcock's aesthetic renewal through European art cinema is also a return to origins, a revitalizing of his own aesthetic by absorbing the work of kindred filmmakers whom he recognized as more daring than he.

The case of Antonioni is particularly resonant in this respect, because the films of Antonioni most appreciated by Hitchcock, *L'Avventura* and *Blow-Up*, undoubtedly bear the imprint of Antonioni's own exposure to Hitchcock. The influence of *Rear Window* on *Blow-Up* is well known.[8] However, *L'Avventura*, too, bears the influence of Hitchcock in its story of a woman who disappears and the relationship that forms in the aftermath between her female friend and former boyfriend. Both *The Lady Vanishes* and *Rear Window* are stories of disappearing women where a couple is formed in the quest to find her. *Vertigo* arguably forms the most explicit template for *L'Avventura*, as the couple is formed in the second half of the film out of their complex relationship to the woman who "disappears" in the first half. Sandro (Gabriele Ferzetti) in *L'Avventura*, like Scottie Ferguson (James Stewart) in *Vertigo*, seeks to re-find his lost love Anna (Lea Massari) in the body of another woman, Claudia (Monica Vitti), and Claudia, like Judy Barton (Kim Novak), seems to uncannily assume the other woman's identity by both wearing her dress and dying her hair. The parallels between the directors are so close that by the time Antonioni makes *L'Avventura*, Hitchcock's *Psycho* (1960) seems to echo its structure, although Hitchcock avoids a romantic relationship between Sam Loomis (John Gavin) and Lila Crane (Vera Miles), the couple who try to find out what happened to the woman who disappeared.

In this essay I will use the complex relationship between Italian art cinema and Hitchcock's films to help illuminate the idea of influence itself. I will begin by framing how any specific idea or account of influence takes place against a backdrop of broader aesthetic norms. The aesthetic strategies of art cinema and the figure of the "wandering woman," who is often a focal point of those strategies, are an already familiar part of Hitchcock's aesthetic, but they are tempered by the constraints and norms of classical narration. In his encounter with Italian cinema, and in particular, Antonioni's *L'Avventura*, Hitchcock found those strategies reflected back to him anew. However, if a convincing case for influence is to be established, it is important to track precise connections between films, and this is what I undertake in the second section of the essay. Having thereby grounded the idea of influence in particular renderings of the *mise-en-scène* of the wandering woman, I develop a more abstract, thematic affinity between the works based upon their shared exploration, through the figure of the wandering woman, of a migratory "mimetic" desire, as theorized by René Girard. Again, my argument is that mimetic desire was already a feature of Hitchcock's work, but the lesson of *L'Avventura* allows him to pursue a peculiarly abstract, and therefore self-conscious, representation of this desire in *The Birds*. *The Birds* is well known for its experimental electronic soundtrack, but this too, I argue, is partially inspired by Antonioni's use of sound in *L'Avventura*, in a manner that supports the articulation of mimetic desire. In this, Hitchcock's encounter with Italian art cinema and *L'Avventura* in particular thus sets the stage for the renewal of Hitchcock's aesthetic in *The Birds* that launched the final phase of his career in the 1960s, though that renewal failed to be sustained as the decade wore on.

Art Cinema, and the Wandering Woman

The concept of "art cinema" is often used to refer to something that is historically specific to European films of the 1960s and, canonically, to the works of Bergman, Fellini and Antonioni, as in the term "European art cinema." Using European film of the 1960s as a reference point, David Bordwell, in a seminal essay, abstracted art cinema into a set of characteristic traits.[9] These are, broadly: the dedramatization of narrative through such strategies as the loosening of cause and effect and the increased role assigned to chance (objective realism); the investigation and reflection upon character psychology, which may be linked to the direct representation of a character's mental states (subjective realism); and the overt, intrusive presence of a narrator who frames the story. These strategies further entail a flexible use of style that is not subservient to its role in advancing the plot but can serve expressivity or narrational commentary; they also foster narrative ambiguity as an end itself of the art film, where the meaning of what we see and hear is purposively indeterminate and the narrative ends unresolved. Art cinema is contrasted, in Bordwell's definition, to classical narrative cinema, which is tightly plotted, uses style as a transparent vehicle for communicating plot, and is action-centered, objective, unambiguous, and unselfconscious.

Bordwell argues that the protagonist of art cinema is often an individual in a state of mental and spiritual alienation and cast in a passive, reactive relationship to his environment. This character is often depicted as a male protagonist in canonical films of European modernism, such as Fellini's *8½* (1960) or Antonioni's *The Passenger* (1975), but Mark Betz has helpfully drawn attention to the pervasive presence of what he calls "the wandering women" in European Cinema of the late 1950s and early 1960s, especially in the films of Antonioni.[10] The wandering woman walks alone through a landscape, whether city or country, without clear-cut purpose, both looking and being looked at, or if she has a purpose, we don't know what it is. The term "wandering woman" captures the connection in works of European art cinema between female presence in the public sphere and the presumption of sexual availability. For example, in Antonioni's cinema she is usually in the process of leaving a relationship, as in *L'Eclisse* (*The Eclipse*, 1962), or has temporarily left her man, as in *La Notte* (*The Night*, 1961) in a manner that exposes her to the often unwanted gaze of male strangers and to the threat of sexual assault. The sexuality of the wandering woman is, in this way, dramatized through Antonioni's plots, but it is equally rendered through performance, by the self-conscious manner in which her sexuality is acted for and captured by the camera that tracks her with intimacy in public space.

The origins of the wandering woman lie in the figure of the prostitute as "street-walker," as she is represented, for example, in Weimar Cinema, in a figure like Pabst's Lulu. Murnau, too, evokes this connection with his vampish "woman of the city" in *Sunrise*, though she does not get paid for sex, so in this sense she anticipates the figure of the wandering woman. For the wandering woman, unlike the prostitute, is endowed with a bourgeois subjectivity that renders her physical wandering and openness to sexuality permissible, even as it subjects her to the threat of sexual assault. This connection is explicitly invoked by Hitchcock himself in the bifurcated halves of *Vertigo*, where Judy Barton recalls the figure of the prostitute, and Madeleine Elster, the epitome of the wandering woman, is her bourgeois avatar. The connection of the bourgeois wandering woman to the prostitute is also explicitly made by Antonioni in *L'Avventura* when the male protagonist, whose affections have already migrated from one wandering woman to another (Anna to Claudia), pays an American starlet for casual sex near the conclusion of the film.

The figure of the wandering woman in European art cinema is significant both in terms of narrative form and visual representation or style. The "wandering" of the female protagonist contributes to the aleatory character of that cinema: the wandering woman drifts; she is a character who encounters and reacts to experiences. Antonioni's films also evoke a particular kind of art-house sexuality wherein the female characters, while they may perform for a third party in the fiction, seem always to be on display for the gaze of the camera, as if their very existence or life as a character depended on that gaze. In Antonioni, as in *Vertigo*, the wandering of the wandering woman is linked to the expressivity of pure cinema, or cinema without verbal language, in which narration takes place through sound and image, freeing the representation of space and time in film from the dramaturgical constraints of the "talkie" and creating a space for connotation, ambiguity, and the representation of subjectivity. Antonioni realizes these Hitchcockian concerns far beyond Hitchcock's own achievements and provided him a new vocabulary for articulating them.

This staging of the female figure is connected in the work of Antonioni and other European directors with the close relationship they developed with their female muses: Bergman and Liv Ullman, Antonioni and Monica Vitti, De Sica and Sophia Loren, Rossellini and Ingrid Bergman, Godard and Anna Karina. Though Sophia Loren and Ingrid Bergman were established stars, in the other cases, the omnipotent director plucks the actress out of obscurity and literally fashions her image, especially her face, as an object of devotion for the gaze of the camera. At the same time, these actresses manifest a different kind of to-be-looked-at-ness than the carefully manufactured and manicured beauty of the Hollywood star. Monica Vitti projects at once an air of naturalness, spontaneity or playfulness and a mask-like illegibility that bespeaks a certain brittleness or vulnerability. Vitti's eyes are completely restless, and her body is constantly in motion, full of life, even as she is relentlessly watched, modeled, framed, and even boxed in by Antonioni's camera. Her aura is at once remote, sophisticatedly modern, and intensely vulnerable.

How does Hitchcock's cinema relate to and depart from the idioms of art cinema, and what are the distinctive features of *The Birds* that can be traced to art cinema? In general, Hitchcock works broadly within tightly structured, objective, action-centered, classical narration, but sews into that narration a heightened level of narrative ambiguity created by an unreliably communicative narrator; he also manifests a marked level of stylistic self-consciousness in order to layer a level of connotation upon narrative verisimilitude. While Hitchcock allows the romance to be realized and the perverse obstacles ranged against it to be overcome, he simultaneously delights in the frustration of romance and the allure of human perversity through his manipulation of style and form in a manner that was influenced by German expressionism. Hitchcock's pervasive ambiguity is highlighted by the frequency with which he struggled over the ending of his films, many of which conclude on an uncertain note. These formal traits of Hitchcock's work allow his films both to inhabit and subvert the idiom of the Hollywood melodrama, the story of the formation of the couple.

The Birds is consistent with Hitchcock's broader cinema but amplifies certain traits in a manner that demonstrates Hitchcock's exposure to art cinema. It foregrounds style in a manner that exceeds narrative meaning both in terms of the visual orchestration of camera movement and *mise-en-scène*, which tracks the looks of characters, orchestrates their gestures, places them in space, and follows their movements through space; and in terms of the soundtrack, which eschews a score and utilizes electronic audio to render the sound of the birds. It dedramatizes the human story both by dwelling on relatively banal events in the lives of its characters and rendering those events that are not intrinsically commonplace banal relative to the destruction and chaos wrought by the bird attacks. Finally, it consistently invites us to meditate on meaning by creating and sustaining pervasive ambiguity around why the birds attack, an ambiguity that was systematically inserted into the script by Evan Hunter, Hitchcock, and his writing consultants who sought to intimate but not to cement an explanation that linked the bird attacks to the human story.[11] In addition, all these traits of the narrative are organized around the representation of the subjectivity and sexual agency of a wandering woman. Melanie Daniels, a society playgirl, enters into a whimsical mating game with a lawyer, Mitch Brenner (Rod Taylor), whom she encountered in a bird shop in San Francisco, and descends upon his mother's house with a pair of love-birds in a manner that coincides with, and perhaps provokes, the assault of the birds. *The Birds* concludes not simply ambiguously, but with an ending that is open. The bird attacks have abated, and the Brenner family with Melanie leave the homestead as we watch dawn rise "over-the-shoulder" of the quiescent birds that remain behind. Will the birds attack again? There is no "the end," just the Universal logo.

It should be noted from the outset that Hitchcock's wandering woman broadly differs from how the wandering woman is represented in, for example, the films of Antonioni. If we consider only her incarnations from *Vertigo* onward, she is a figure who is possessed with agency, unlike the character of Lidia (Jeanne Moreau) in *La Notte*, for example, or Vittoria (Monica Vitti) in *L'Eclisse*, who seem to wander without a clear-cut purpose. However, her agency is a secret one, whose motive, directly or indirectly, is sexual. In *Vertigo*, Madeleine, although she appears to be the embodiment of the aimlessly wandering woman, is in fact wandering for a precise purpose: to seduce Scottie Ferguson and fulfill Gavin Elster's plot. In *Psycho*, Marion Crane is stealing for love; in *The Birds*, Melanie Daniels is playfully hunting down her man; and in *Marnie* (1964) the "frigid" heroine, also played by Tippi Hedren, is acting to subvert patriarchal authority by stealing from her rich male employers. In these films, Hitchcock's female protagonists thematize the sexual enigma of the wandering woman as a distinctive, if perverse, form of agency.[12] Since they are possessed with agency, these characters nominally conform to the norms of classical narration, yet they are arguably more subversive in their roles than the heroines of

Antonioni's cinema, who, in their lack of agency, are sexually adrift and therefore susceptible to the next available man.

Finally, Hitchcock's relationship to Tippi Hedren is comparable to the relationship of European auteurs to their female stars and arguably partly inspired by them. Of course Hitchcock always "fetishized" his female stars such as Ingrid Bergman and Grace Kelly, though they were shared with other directors. Tippi Hedren was different: her screen persona was profoundly shaped by Hitchcock. He played Pygmalion to her Galatea. And perhaps the nature of her on-screen presence was only intensified by Hitchcock's alleged obsession with and harassment of her, a point to which I shall return. As Joe McElhaney points out, Hedren's image is a curious hybrid between the art cinema actress and the old-fashioned Hollywood star.[13] Hedren, like Vitti, knows she is being watched and is acting for the camera. In *The Birds*, Hitchcock's camera dwells upon her face, her body, and her movement through space, and she in turn seems constantly attuned to its presence. Yet Hedren, by comparison to Vitti, is much more brittle and stiffly artificial: she is made up and accessorized with a studio look that is far from the naturalism of Vitti's glamorously unvarnished image. Yet Hedren's touch-me-not quality, together with the aforementioned narrative agency of her character, bestows upon her screen presence a certain strength and autonomy that hints at sexual androgyny. Hitchcock exploits this aspect of Hedren in *Marnie*, where her character arrogates what is in certain respects a "male" role, and she must be "cured" of her gender confusion and straightened out.

There is one scene in *The Birds*, analyzed at length by Raymond Bellour, where Melanie Daniels, the wandering woman from the city, descends upon the country to seduce the man who lives across the water.[14] This sequence dramatizes the relationship between narrative de-dramatization, excessive stylization, the sexualized figuration of the wandering woman, and interpretative ambiguity in the film. It is undoubtedly important to the story that Melanie delivers the love-birds to Mitch, for it at once re-connects the couple and isolates them in the country, setting the stage for the birds' attack. However, the inordinate attention Hitchcock gives to this sequence is peculiar. Narratively speaking, Melanie's wandering deflates our expectations. The sequence rhetorically yields a sense of mystery and intrigue, especially through Hitchcock's extensive deployment of point-of-view editing together with a moving camera, but the payoff is minor: when will Mitch spot Melanie? It is also artificially prolonged in the chase around the bay. We are simply invited to "bird watch" — and what better alibi for bird watching than artful filmmaking — as Melanie swoops across the bay, creeps into the house, and retreats to her perch in the boat. The first bird attack that hits Melanie as she closes on Mitch in the boat is also a dramatic anticlimax that raises, above all, an interpretative conundrum: why did the bird attack her? If the bird attack does seem to be an "answer" to a provocation induced by Melanie's sexual presence and in particular her gaze, it is wholly at the level of symbolism or connotation.

Establishing Influence: La Ciociara,
L'Avventura, *and* The Birds

In Vittorio De Sica's film *La Ciociara* (*Two Women*), made in 1960, Cesira (Sophia Loren) and her thirteen-year old daughter Rosetta (Eleonora Brown), deracinated by the war, are traveling like many other refugees through the Italian countryside and take shelter in a church, where they are attacked and gang-raped by a band of marauding Moroccan allied soldiers. There is some scattered dialogue but it is a sequence that is largely without it. The scene is strikingly echoed in the extended sequence of "pure cinema" that forms the climax of *The Birds*, and which was, notoriously, as harrowing for the actor as it is for the spectator. Melanie Daniels, feeling the presence of the birds, climbs upstairs to the attic bedroom to confront her adversaries, only to be trapped inside and viciously assaulted by them. The telling detail that binds the two scenes

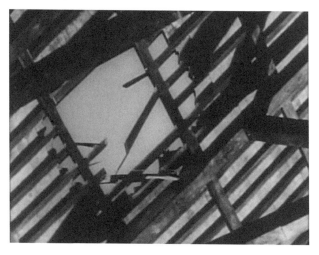

Figure 1

is a hole, a breach, in the church roof, which Rosetta looks up to prior to the assault as she hears the sounds of birds (fig. 1). The hole is exactly replicated by Hitchcock as a breach in the roof of the attic (fig. 2) through which the birds enter to assault Melanie (and the spectator).

The scene from *Two Women* dramatizes the risk of sexual predation posed to the woman who wanders in public space. It is laden with metaphor. It takes place in a church—architectural analogue of the bodies of the women—the older of whom is doubled by her virginal daughter, Rosetta. The hole in the roof is like a wound in the body of the church. As the sound of birds heard by Rosetta meld with the noise of Cesira moving wooden furniture, there is an echo effect motivated by the chamber of the church. Yet, given the girl's semi-conscious state and the off-screen, "acousmatic," nature of the bird sounds, these sounds take on a psychological resonance. The hole, in conjunction with the sounds of birds, prefigure Rosetta's violation as marauding swarms of manic, feverish, savage, wide-eyed, dark-skinned soldiers overrun the church. At the conclusion of the sequence the sound of the birds returns as Cesira, awakening, looks up at the hole and

Figure 2

down to Rosetta's prostrate body. The violation of the women within this setting is linked to the Passion of Christ as Rosetta lies on the floor after the rape, as if crucified, in front of a statue that appears to be a pieta on one side and a desecrated altar on the other. Her mother functions as a surrogate spectator, a helpless onlooker to her suffering, until she herself is knocked out and violated. De Sica recognizes, here, Christ's Passion as the primal scene of melodrama, which is transposed to the body of the virginal woman as the incarnation of persecuted innocence.

In Hitchcock's film, the "acousmatic" sound track of the birds as an aural blanket is writ large in the film, as I have analyzed in detail elsewhere.[15] While Hitchcock had deployed figurations of bird sounds both aurally and symbolically in previous work, the significance of this scene for Hitchcock in which the sound of birds foreshadow a gang rape cannot be overstated. In the attic scene itself, the birds are silent until they attack, but other aspects of De Sica's *mise-en-scène* are salient. The bedroom is a charged space in Hitchcock's world, both a childhood sanctuary and the place of sexual secrets. As one who has lost her mother, Melanie identifies with the daughter Cathy Brenner (Veronica Cartwright) in the Brenner household, and she will become a daughter in the Brenner house by marrying Mitch. Her entry into the girl's bedroom is a return to a sanctuary of innocence where she will confront

Figure 3

Figure 4

the birds in her most vulnerable state. Like the daughter in *La Ciociara*, Melanie looks upon a hole in the roof that prefigures her own violation, as, in the next moment squawking, beady-eyed birds, who have pecked out the opening and poured through it, now fly forth from the white sheeted frame of a little four-poster bed and start pecking and fluttering her to pieces. De Sica's film depicts an actual rape that is laden with religious symbolism; Hitchcock's film depicts a symbolic rape, through the figuration of the birds, which is presented as martyrdom. Melanie, by knowingly entering the space, seems to offer herself to the birds in a Christ-like sacrifice, and the birds peck her hands, creating stigmata.

Figure 5

Figure 6

In *L'Avventura*, Anna has gone missing during a short vacation jaunt on a Mediterranean Island. As Sandro and Claudia try to make sense of her absence, they fall into a relationship. Sandro has just entered a hotel, following a lead that Anna might be staying there, while Claudia stands outside against a stone balustrade in a closed frame. As she looks to the right (fig. 3), the frame opens to reveal a string of leering men perched on the steps (fig. 4). Feeling uncomfortable she moves away. Looking back and up again (fig. 5), she sees dozens more men lined up along a low stone wall bordering a raised *piazza* (fig 6). The scene is a striking prefiguration of the moment in *The Birds* when, as Melanie nonchalantly smokes her

Figure 7

Figure 8

cigarette in front of a jungle gym, the birds slowly and silently gather behind her, their presence known only to the audience. Then as she looks up to follow the flight of a single bird, we discover, shockingly, that the birds have gathered *en masse* behind her (fig. 7) and she reacts in trepidation (fig. 8).

The scene from *L'Avventura* dramatizes sexual predation in public urban space, and it supports the interpretation of Hitchcock's birds as a figuration of a predatory sexual drive writ large and abstracted. It also suggests an ambiguous psychological motivation for their presence. As Claudia casts her gaze wider, the staring men proliferate to absurd proportions. They are not mere figments of her imagination, yet they also represent a horrific projection of her own anxiety and shame over having entered so precipitously into an affair with the partner of her missing friend. She is tainted in her own eyes, and as she stands and wanders alone in the square, she is represented like a prostitute in the way she is a magnet for the licentious gaze of men. In the jungle gym scene in *The Birds*, it also seems as if the presence of the birds has been conjured into being. This effect is created by the mantra of the song sung by the children in the school house, "Risseldy-rosseldy," that emanates from a source that is entirely off-screen, and therefore seems to inhabit a space that is as much mental as physical.[16] It is not Hitchcock's purpose for us to simply interpret the birds as a psychological projection; rather his purpose, like Antonioni's, is to sow a psychological resonance and ambiguity into the scene.

In fact, the jungle gym scene arguably condenses both the influence of De Sica and Antonioni on Hitchcock's film. For the rapacious soldiers in the attack on the women, shot by De Sica from a high angle, swarm like the flock of birds that attack Melanie and the children. De Sica, like Hitchcock, creates suspense by cutting from the unknowing victim to the gathering attackers, and in both cases the wandering woman is aligned with the figure of the child to whom she also becomes a mother, thereby establishing her essential innocence. Furthermore, the racial (not to say racist) connotations of beady-eyed dark-skinned soldiers raping white women in De Sica's film resonate with the racial overtones of the bird attacks in Hitchcock's film. As John Hellman has shown, *The Birds* is a film replete with contextual references to the Kennedy era, including the black struggle over civil rights and white anxiety over black empowerment.[17] Although black birds mix with seagulls in the bedroom attack, it is beady-eyed black crows that gather on the "jungle" gym and attack Melanie and the children in an earlier scene. In this respect the jungle gym scene uncomfortably invokes, at a distance, the racial melodrama that, as Linda Williams has argued, long informed the depiction of white-black relationships in America.[18] Furthermore, in this scene, Hitchcock is particularly attentive to the acousmatic sound of the birds. Just as the natural sounds of the birds in *Two Women* blend with the echo effect of the moving furniture and evoke a sense

Figure 9

that the swarming soldiers are the realization of a nightmare, so too the gathering of the birds at the jungle gym, "accompanied" by the children's song, seem conjured into being.

André Bazin wrote of Hitchcock, for him "it is always a question of creating in the *mise-en-scène*, starting from the scenario, but mainly by the expressionism of the framing, the lighting, or the relation of the characters to the décor, an essential instability of image."[19] This "instability" is also characteristic of the scenes from *La Ciociara* and *L'Avventura* but it serves different functions. In De Sica's film the "instability" of the frame is captured in a high-angle shot in which a shaft of light penetrates the vault of the church to touch the prone women just prior to the emergence of the shadowed figures of the rapists in the foreground, where it is clearly motivated as an anticipation of the impending rape (fig. 9). However, in *L'Avventura,* the instability that characterizes the framing of Claudia in relationship to the gathering men above her is more enigmatic: is the threat real or imagined, and how are we to interpret what is taking place? This kind of "instability" that is an index of ambiguity pervades Antonioni's film and profoundly influences the design of framing and *mise-en-scène* in *The Birds*.

Figure 10

Figure 11

The Birds is replete with portentous off-screen gazes that suggest a significance that exceeds narrative context. One example is where Annie stands at the mailbox in an avian posture (fig. 10). The instability in the image is created by the gaze off screen, the way Annie is thrust into the foreground relative to the receding fences, the obtruding mailbox, and the red against white and gray composition, as well as the way in which the shot is enigmatically held beyond the time necessary to convey narrative information. This kind of enigmatic self-consciously posed shot is common, even ubiquitous, in Antonioni. This image in *The Birds* directly recalls a shot in which Claudia and Sandro react in profile to the sound of a boat off the island (fig. 11)—perhaps it could be

Figure 12

Figure 13

a clue to Anna's presence? The off-screen sound motivates Claudia's glance as she turns from looking left to looking right, and yet the shot itself is self-consciously posed. Claudia's neck is sharply turned and her hair blows about her face, giving her profile a statuesque power and intensity, and a presence that is charged with sexualized tension that exceeds narrative denotation. Earlier in the film Antonioni configures a group profile shot where the bourgeois characters, quite out of place on the island and especially now as they are confronted with a sense of threat, are depicted in posed manner looking left in profile toward Sandro as he decides what they should do (fig. 12). This kind of group profile shot is recalled in the highly posed shot in the Tides restaurant as Melanie,

Figure 14

Figure 15

Mitch, and the fisherman in the diner look out of the window off-screen right at the impending bird attack (fig. 13).

A third example of this kind of unstable composition in *L'Avventura* is when Claudia, framed at extreme low angle, witnesses Anna's love-making (fig. 14). Since Claudia has already spied them making love through the window this information is essentially redundant, but it is shot with an uncommon attention to composition, which gives the scene a portentous significance that exceeds any straightforward meaning: why should she be so concerned with the idea that Anna is having sex with him? The composition of this shot is recalled precisely in Hitchcock's portrayal of the response of Melanie (fig. 15) and the others to the

Figure 16

birdss departure from the Brenner household after their vicious final massed assault. Now it is certainly true that this is a significant moment in *The Birds*. The radically low angle employed by Hitchcock serves to articulate the connection between the birds' departure and reactions of the characters to their leaving, and yet the way the characters are photographed again seems to carry a meaning that exceeds narrative context as they loom in front of the camera.

A fourth example of framing and posture that directly inspired Hitchcock is the scene near the conclusion of *L'Avventura* where Claudia, waking up early in the morning, alone and anxious her hotel room since Sandro has not returned from the party, visits her friend Patrizia (Esmeralda Ruspoli) in search of him. She appears in extreme long shot at the end of the corridor and runs its full length in high-heeled shoes, her arms flailing to the side until she arrives near the camera in low-angle full shot, at which point she veers off to a door on the right that she enters (fig. 16). This shot is overtly expressive: the *mise-en-scène* of the hallway and her traversal of it register the character's sense of anxiety. The shot is echoed in *The Birds* in the scene where Lydia, having discovered Dan Fawcett with his eyes pecked out, rushes headlong down a narrow corridor (fig. 17) and then down the path from the house in her high-heels, her arms flailing, and her footsteps resounding on the stone from the heels of her shoes. The sense of

Figure 17

urgency and anxiety is intensified in a manner that is appropriate to context, yet what this scene also emphasizes is Hitchcock's fascination, via Antonioni, with a distinctively feminine mode of comportment that here is ruffled beyond measure.

Wandering Women and Migrating, Mimetic Desire

From his earliest period, Hitchcock was interested in exploring the ramifications of incipiently murderous triangular relationships, such as between Daisy (June), her detective boyfriend Joe (Malcolm Chandler), and the eponymous character (played by Ivor Novello) in *The Lodger*, or in the triangles formed amongst the protagonists of *The Ring* and *The Manxman*. Furthermore, Hitchcock was always fascinated with implicating the spectator through the gaze of the camera in a scene of sexual intimacy that is rendered "perverse" by the fact of spying. Hitchcock spoke of the camera itself as the third party in a *ménàge a trois* when he discussed the kissing scene in *Notorious* with Truffaut, however the camera is also often allied to the third party within a triangular relationship who acts as a spy-witness within the scene.[20] For example, there is a moment in *The Lodger* when the viewer, alongside the protagonist of the film encounters policeman Joe playfully handcuffing the woman both men love, Daisy, at the bottom of a staircase, in a manner that enacts two triangles that depend upon whether we construe the Lodger as a rescuer or murderer. In *Rebecca*, we are privileged witnesses to a bedroom scene, where Mrs. Danvers presses the fur of Rebecca's coat to the cheek of the second Mrs. de Winter until the latter recoils in horror, in this case establishing of scene of intimate rivalry both between Danvers and the second Mrs. de Winter for Rebecca and between Danvers/Rebecca and the second Mrs. de Winter for de Winter and Manderley.

Antonioni's cinema takes these Hitchcockian concerns to a new level of sophistication. Antonioni enters into an erotic complicity with his actresses, particularly Monica Vitti. In this erotic complicity, Vitti performs for the camera's gaze and allows her subjectivity to be circumscribed by that gaze. Antonioni's female actors, thus defined in their sexuality by the camera, provoke the desire of male characters in the film as if the erotic identity that is produced in their performance for the camera has the capacity to enter into the world of the fiction. Furthermore, within the fictional world, Antononi's women provoke male desire through their erotic rivalry or competition with other women, which Antonioni stages with a frankness and lack of prurience that eluded Hitchcock. Finally, through strategies of art cinema narration, Antonioni represents desire as an abstract force of nature that exceeds the will of any one character: the figure of the wandering woman in *L'Avventura* both embodies and catalyzes a desire that exceeds her own agency, and her wandering becomes, as it were, the vehicle of an impersonal migratory desire that seems to pass from character to character. Inspired by Antonioni, *The Birds* is remarkably frank in its representation of female sexual agency. It registers the rivalrous desire between female sexual rivals, and quite self-consciously represents this rivalrous desire as an abstract force of nature.

In both Antonioni and Hitchcock, the nature of this rivalrous intimacy and the desire it elicits can arguably be explained in terms of what Girard has termed "mimetic" desire, that is, a desire that arises from imitation. The crucial idea behind Girard's theory of mimetic desire is that it is a form of desire that does not originate with the agent who desires but is imitated from someone else in a way that the imitating agent is usually unaware of. There is always an initial figure, whom Girard terms the "mediator," who desires someone, and this desire of the mediator brings into being or authenticates the sexual longing of his or her rival.[21] However, the mediator's desire is an arbitrary starting point for the migration or transmission of mimetic desire, for the mediator's desire will itself be based upon another's desire; in this sense mimetic desire for Girard already exists. It is an anthropological constant that arises from a condition of competition and rivalry. Mimetic desire is contagious or viral not only in the way that it seems to circulate from one person to another, but that it also has an incipiently deadly quality because it is born out of rivalry and promotes conflict as the rival become the model and the model the rival.

The theory suggests a triangle of agents: the mediator, the person who has caught the desire, and the love object. However, Girard argues that the triangle of mimetic desire is one that does not in fact require three people. Making reference to Jean Paul Sartre's influential theory of desire in *Being and Nothingness*, he argues that there is an asymmetry between self and other in sexual desire, because when I desire you sexually, I desire to possess your subjectivity in and through your body.[22] If you allow my desire for your body to become the model for your desire, your desire will take the form of narcissism, or to use the old-fashioned word used by Girard himself to refer to female narcissism, "coquetry"; thus, you yourself will become a rival in my desire for you and we will be enslaved in a contagious double-bind. "The coquette," writes Girard, "does not wish to surrender her precious self to the desire that she arouses, but were she not to provoke it she would not feel so precious The favor she finds in her own eyes is based exclusively on the favor with which she is regarded by Others. For this reason the coquette is constantly looking for proofs of this favor; she encourages and stirs up her lover's desires, not in order to give herself to him but to enable her the better to refuse him."[23]

While the term "coquette" (or its more modern equivalent, "flirt") lacks the right nuance to characterize the screen presence of the wandering woman, and while I do not think that Sartre's and Girard's theories are convincing as a general theory of desire, Girard's theory nevertheless provides a revision of the traditional understanding of the to-be-looked-at woman in film theory and an interesting gloss on the role of the wandering woman as an instigator of mimetic desire.[24] Within the fiction of *L'Avventura*, female characters display different degrees of flirtatiousness, but all the female actors—Monica Vitti especially—enter into a special relationship with Antonioni's camera. Where the female actor exists in this way to be loved by the camera itself and the spectator who shares the gaze of the camera, she is defined by this relationship. No interaction with her is possible that could break the shell of objectification, for as we imagine ourselves to look upon the face and body of the actress, the world of the film is screened off from the onlooker to whom the actress presents herself in the manner described by Stanley Cavell.[25] The pretext for the representation of mimetic desire is created out of the chemistry or alchemy of the female actor's performance in front of the gaze of the camera. The female figure thus constituted is not the to-be-looked-at figure passively constituted under the gaze of the camera as she is described in traditional film theory; she is the actress who desires to please the camera. Her to-be-looked-at-ness is provocative: it is the product of her own performative agency, and it elicits a contagion of mimetic desire prior to any agency she might bear as a character in the story. The qualities of the actress before the camera are transferred to the character within the fiction and everyone she encounters becomes, as it were, her potential rival/lover. Of course, female agency does not have to be represented as narcissistic, though this is very common in cinema; nor does this representation need to be linked to desire's contagion, though that is what Antonioni, and both before and after him, Hitchcock, seek to explore.

L'Avventura opens with a wandering woman, Anna, walking along a driveway away from the house. Framed in long shot, she begins to approach the camera and when she is in medium shot the camera begins to track back with her at a slightly low angle. She appears strong and independent, though sullen and brooding, walking with some purpose, though we do not know what that purpose is. She arrives outside the villa to encounter her father, whom she says she was looking for in the bedroom, and they proceed to have an exchange that establishes his jealous guardianship of her, even as she makes clear that she has no intention of marrying the man she plan to meet and go sailing with to the Aoelian islands on a short holiday. Anna is immediately established as an active, provocative, and perhaps rather capricious sexual agent.

Melanie's introduction in *The Birds* is comparable, though more elaborate. *The Birds* opens with Melanie Daniels walking confidently and with purpose across a street in San Francisco as we hear the sound of gulls. As the camera tracks her along the pavement to the front of a bird shop, we hear the squawk of a bird, then immediately afterwards a wolf whistle made by a boy, to which she turns and responds, which is again followed by a squawk as she looks up into the sky at the circling birds. Economically, in the style of Hollywood narration, this opening shot establishes the wandering woman as a figure of desirable female sexuality: she is a "dolly bird" in cockney slang, or in a slightly difference sense a "love-bird." Her desirability is marked by the wolf whistle that nominally issues from the boy who passes in the foreground, and which she can interpret in a benign and playful way because he is so young. But her gaze back towards him is just off-center, and because the boy passes so quickly it is as if the whistle could be issuing from off-screen behind the camera's gaze. When she turns slightly to look up at the birds circling in the sky, it is again as if she is looking up and over at a direction that is "behind" the camera, which is then filled in the reverse field shot by the circling birds. In this way, the contagion of an alluring and incipiently deadly desire is sparked by the gaze of the camera as it brings into being the figure of the wandering woman, whose sexuality is metaphorically linked at once to love-birds and to the death birds.[26]

Following Anna's introduction in *L'Avventura*, she meets Claudia and the two women speed into town in an open top sports car to meet Sandro; Anna repairs alone to his room. As Anna and Sandro begin to make love, they are watched by Claudia in the plaza downstairs through an open window, and then overheard by her from an art gallery below, as Antonioni cuts to close shots of their lovemaking. Claudia's complicit gaze creates a triangulation of desire and bestows upon this lovemaking an illicit quality, which is passed on to the point of view of the camera that shares her third-party gaze. Furthermore, a sense of sexualized suspense is created, first by the little detail of Claudia swinging her handbag like a pendulum as she is framed through the window as she waits for Anna, then by her restless, fidgety motion as she moves into and out of the art gallery.

The two women continue to be linked together as intimates and rivals in desire through a parallel structure in the *mise-en-scène*. When Anna enters Sandro's apartment, she steps onto the balcony with the Po River as backdrop in a manner that suggests her rising desire. Claudia then passes through the art gallery during their lovemaking and steps onto the balcony below the open window of the lovers' room to occupy a similar position against the backdrop and sound of the rushing water. She then looks up to the open window of the storey above as we see Anna's face turn enigmatically away and upward during her lovemaking as if in response to Claudia's gaze. The scenes evoke a connection, a transference of desire, which is completed later when, after Anna has disappeared, Claudia joins Sandro in his search for her and they make love in the open air, while the camera dwells now on Claudia's face as it had on Anna's earlier. Nominally Anna models Claudia's desire because Sandro becomes Claudia's love object after Anna's disappearance, yet Anna is openly enamored of Claudia's beauty.

This triangulation of desire is echoed in another, much later, scene in the film in which Giulia (Dominique Blanchar), frustrated in marriage, courts seduction by a seventeen-year-old artist in the villa of an aristocratic friend surrounded by overtly erotic primitive art and in the presence of Claudia, who, bereft of Sandro, is isolated, anxious, and bored. Although Giulia allows herself to be seduced by the boy, she is equally flirtatious toward Claudia, whom she coaxes to witness the seduction. Again, nominally, Giulia models Claudia's desire, since Guila's transgressive sexual behavior seems to inspire Claudia to overcome her reticence and make love with Sandro, yet at the same time Giulia, following Anna, admires Claudia's beauty. The fact that the triangle is in this way repeated establishes the migratory, contagious nature of the desire that circulates among the women.

Prior to Anna's disappearance, Claudia and Anna go on the boat trip to the Aeolian Islands, where the women are drawn close together as the passengers on the boat are forced to invade each other's personal space, and the camera too presses into uncomfortable proximity. First we witness a mildly suggestive conversation between Claudia and Anna. Playfully swinging to and fro while holding onto a vertical pole, Anna looks into Claudia's eyes as they discuss how they had been happily rocked to sleep, while in front of her in the foreground the angled torso of a prone male sunbather who slept very badly contributes at once to form a triangle and to create a profound imbalance or tension in the composition of the frame. Then, after Anna has returned from her swim in order to escape, she alleges, the presence of a shark, she retreats with Claudia to the cabin to change; here they are framed in a tight medium two-shot from behind. Antonioni cuts to a close-up of Claudia saying enigmatically "Well, what is it?" Anna invades the frame from below and looks up into her eyes. As Claudia looks down at Anna indulgently and enigmatically, Claudia slips off her dress (though we might initially mistake her own hand on the strap of her slip for Anna's) while Anna rocks back in laughter. Then, framed in a tight close-up two-shot, Claudia decides to try on her dress. Subsequently, both women who are naked with their backs to the camera get dressed, and Anna makes her secret confession that she lied about seeing a shark that caused her to leave the water. Whereas the lovemaking scene near the opening of the film positions the spectator's gaze upon the lovers through the look of a character (Claudia), here the cabin door in the rear of the *mise-en-scène* is closed, creating the sense of a sealed enclosure that exists for the audience's eyes only. Antonioni plays upon and amplifies the idea of the camera, both as the third party in a *ménage à trois*, and as a participant in an invasion of privacy, in a manner that at once invokes and surpasses Hitchcock's own rendering of such a *mise-en-scène*.

The Birds triangulates mimetic desire in way that seems modeled upon *L'Avventura*. In *The Birds* the affair between the brunette, Annie Hayworth, who has the Americanized name of Antonioni's protagonist, Anna, and Mitch is already over. Thus though Annie is broody like Anna, her demeanor has a more conventional motivation as the jilted lover. However, the fact that the plot of *The Birds* contrives to have her hang around Bodega Bay in spite of her failed romance leads to her becoming a triangulating force in Melanie's desire. Their first encounter occurs prior to the scene in which Melanie delivers the love-birds to Mitch Brenner. Melanie swoops down to Bodega Bay in an open top sports car, which recalls the association between sexually active women and the sports cars in *L'Avventura*. On the pretext of finding out the name of Mitch Brenner's little sister, she is sent to Annie's house. She pauses in front of the schoolhouse before drawing up in front of Annie's house with an assertive spurt of the car engine. Hitchcock frames the car so that it provocatively dominates the frame as if asserting Melanie's claim upon Annie's territory in the manner of a sexual rival. As Melanie leaves, Annie leans on the car framed by a closed red U.S. mail box (it is Melanie who is now delivering the mail to Mitch) and declares, "I am rather an open book, I am afraid, or rather a closed one," intimating the state of her relationship to Mitch, and as she does so the love-birds tweet. She looks down at them as Melanie tells her they are love-birds. "Oh, I see" Annie responds as they exchange knowing glances across them. Of course, we could not possibly mistake Annie and Melanie for the love-birds, but they share the "tweet-tweets" of love-birds, and the gender of love-birds is ambiguous; indeed, they look identical. Later in the film, the knowing child, Cathy, explicitly comments on the implications of their identical appearance: "Is there a man and a woman? I can't tell which is which."

When Melanie returns to Annie's after the encounter with Mitch, she preens at the front door in the glass before Annie appears. As Annie answers it, she leans forward in a posture that accentuates the forward thrust of her breasts towards Melanie, a stance that is at once assertive and alluring. Melanie asks her if she can stay the night (on the implausible assumption that every other room in town is taken) and Annie welcomes her, accompanied by the sound of birds (which Annie draws attention to). In a third scene, Melanie returns after dinner at the Brenners' and they settle down together to an intimate brandy as Annie confesses her relationship to Mitch and her desire to remain near him. Both women light cigarettes that, in the manner they are held, become accessories to their preening femininity. Their conversation is interrupted by a call from Mitch; during this conversation a brooding Annie is first framed in the foreground with Melanie in the background, and then she is framed in reverse field in profile from Melanie's point of view as she remains talking on the phone in a manner that constructs the triangle. After putting the phone down and announcing her invitation to Cathy's birthday party, Melanie pulls out her sole piece of luggage, purchased from the general store—a pink nightgown that she displays for Annie's admiring eyes. As they prepare to say goodnight and Annie gives her blessing for the visit, a gull hits the door for no apparent reason, but as if precipitated from or in response to the contagion of desire. The allure of female sophistication and eroticism is scarcely as effective as Antonioni's portrayal of female sexuality but the contagious sexuality of the wandering women here is surely suggested as desire is, as it were, passed from woman to woman and linked to the onset of the bird attacks.

The Birds, too, has more than one triangle. Many commentators have remarked on the kitchen scene I have already referred to where Lydia confronts Mitch over Melanie as if she were her jealous rival, a rivalry further underscored by the way in which Mitch refers to his mother as "dear."[27] Thus not only is Melanie's desire for Mitch modeled on that of Annie, it is also modeled on Annie's rivalry with Lydia, which the two women discuss, and which is repeated as Melanie becomes the rival of Lydia. The birds, in this respect, have been commonly interpreted as an expression of the rage of the protective, rivalrous, maternal super-ego against the intrusive claimants for Mitch's love, Annie and Melanie. However, Annie's position in the triangle has now been altered with Melanie's arrival on the scene, and is now comparable to that of Lydia. This proliferation of triangles points to the way in which, if the birds are expressive of the negative, incipiently murderous aspect of migratory desire, it is not a desire that can simply be attached to one character but rather passes among all the women.

The link between destructive nature in the form of the birds and Melanie's agency is comparable to the role played by destructive nature in relationship to Anna's agency in *L'Avventura*. I have noted how the rushing water is initially identified with Anna's desire. Anna's temperament in *L'Avventura* is, from the beginning, brooding, restless, narcissistic, and incipiently destructive. The rushing water of the Po suggests the external force of an independent contagious desire that is potentially annihilating in its power. Anna equally has an affinity to the sea whose deadliness is figured by the shark that she purports is lurking in the depth of the ocean and expressed in the "vengeful" nature of the sea swells and storm. The restless desire that Anna sets in motion seems to destroy her, possibly by drowning, but there is ultimately no explanation of her disappearance and the arid space of the ancient volcanic island is itself resonant of death. Melanie's relationship to the birds, while purposively enigmatic, is a good deal more explicit. They attack when she arrives at Bodega Bay and she is explicitly blamed by the "mother hen" in the Tides restaurant. Melanie's temperament, unlike Anna's, is playful and upbeat, yet she is also impulsive, a provocateur. In his comments on Hitchcock's script, V.S. Pritchett suggested that she might have accidentally killed someone as a result of her practical jokes, though this suggestion did not make its way into the film.[28] Melanie is thus both cause and object of the bird attacks, just as in *L'Avventura* Anna is both cause and object of the restless onslaught of nature.

The comparison I have drawn between *The Birds* and *L'Avventura* allows us to see more clearly the way in which the birds manifest a generalized, abstracted mimetic desire that is contagious (it moves from person to person) and migratory (it travels through space). The wandering women in *L'Avventura*, Anna and Claudia, are a figuration of this desire. So too is Melanie Daniels. On the one hand, the bird attacks are unconsciously ranged against the rivals in her desire for a connection with Mitch, Annie, and Lydia, and even Cathy, since Cathy has the maternal relationship that Melanie has lost, as well as the familial relationship to her brother Mitch, which Melanie seeks. Melanie identifies with Cathy but also wishes to occupy her place in the Brenner family. At the same time, the attacks are ultimately ranged against Melanie herself. This is in part an expression of the murderous rivalry of Annie and most of all Lydia towards her. However, when the rivalries within the fiction are stripped away, we are left with the contagion of mimetic desire that is solicited by the construction of the figure of the desiring woman for the camera, whose gaze is at once adoring and "murderous," in William Rothman's telling formulation.[29] The birds are thus the incarnation of the rivalrous gaze purveyed by the camera that is provoked by Hedren/Melanie's enticing but essentially inaccessible presence before it.

In both *L'Avventura* and *The Birds*, the contagion of desire is arrested and a different, more empathic, kind of human relationship emerges in its place. In *L'Avventura*, Claudia enters into a serious relationship with Sandro that is mediated by the presence of Anna, but then having failed to find Anna, the restless Sandro sleeps with the young, promiscuous starlet, Gloria Perkins (Dorothea del Poliolo), whom he had been introduced to by a journalist who had boasted that he most certainly would pay for sex with her if he could afford it. Sandro himself has succumbed to imitative desire, but the fact that he pays for sex with this grand whore-starlet, the rival of all women, seems to bring the chain of desire to a halt. In concrete terms, he has rejected Claudia, but his action allows his relationship with Claudia to be placed beyond the realm of desire and their common loss of Anna to be properly acknowledged for the first time. When she discovers what he has done, she obviously feels deeply betrayed, but she nonetheless reaches out to the abject Sandro through her anger in a maternal gesture of forgiveness that is motivated by an altruistic love based on a sense of shared loss rather than self-centered desire, as they unite in their grief over Anna.

At the conclusion of *The Birds*, when Melanie confronts the birds in the attic, she functions, like the figure of Christ, as a "scapegoat" who is atoning for all sin. The scapegoat is an important figure for Girard, for he or she is the person upon whom all hostility can be symbolically directed by a family or society in a manner that bring about the quiescence of mimetic desire and restores a sense of harmony or peace to the social group.[30] Christ, for Girard, is the paradigmatic scapegoat, and it is fitting that Hitchcock in this scene makes allusions to Christ in a manner that recalls the scapegoating of the Lodger at the hands of the mob in his 1927 film. Melanie must suffer this last extreme manifestation of mimetic desire in the rage of the birds, for it undoes her entrapment as an erotic object in the gaze of the camera and thereby releases her from personifying desire within the fiction. Lydia now no longer needs to conceive of Melanie as her opponent in a sexualized rivalry, and in a conclusion which echoes that of *L'Avventura*, she lightly embraces Melanie in a gesture of love that Melanie acknowledges. Their relationship here is reconstituted as a familial one. Lydia has accessed her feelings of maternal affection, and Melanie has discovered a mother. Even while the future is uncertain, the family group seems set to leave the space of contagion as it moves away from the camera and the space of Hitchcock's film itself.

A Note on Sound

Antonioni's experimentation with the soundtrack of *L'Avventura* and its thematic relationship to the figuration of a contagious desire provided a model for Hitchcock's use of sound and supports a distinctive interpretation of its thematic significance. *L'Avventura* has a composed score, but this musical score actually plays a sporadic role in the film. It is first heard some 30 minutes into the film as an oboe theme that accompanies Anna's disappearance and her friends' search. Scored music recurs at 48 minutes to punctuate the moment when Sandro makes his first overt move on Claudia, and it accompanies the continuing search for Anna, as well as Claudia's subsequent breakdown. It briefly occurs 63 minutes into the film when Claudia and Sandro part, then for a longer duration at 77 minutes when Claudia dresses for a dinner she does not want to go to, and then during Giulia's seduction of the young artist. The oboe theme returns when Claudia discovers Sandro's betrayal at the film's conclusion. The only other music in the film is diegetic sound in the form of a popular song on the radio that Claudia sings along with, and the balalaika orchestra in the film's concluding scene in the hotel.

With minimal scoring, ambient sounds take on a distinctive function. Two kinds of sounds are particularly salient: the sound of water and the sounds that are made by moving vehicles. In the scenes where the women stand on the balconies in front of the Po river, moving water is linked to the onset of a desire that is evoked as being, like the river, an on-rushing movement whose source and destination are unknown but whose presence is all-pervasive. The water that is framed in the background moves from somewhere off-screen left to somewhere off-screen right, but its encompassing presence is signaled by its sound. Furthermore, the fact that both women turn their back on the water that frames their action—Anna to look at Sandro, Claudia to look up at the window where Anna and Sandro make love—in an action that is repeated, suggests that their actions are connected by impersonal force or agency that is embodied by the onrushing water. The theme of water and its connection to female desire is extended in the subsequent boat trip to the Aeolian Islands. The omnipresence of water that surrounds the boat, and subsequently the island which they alight upon, is registered by the sound of its lapping and then surging currents that take the place of any musical accompaniment. The surging sound of the sea is particularly intense in the scenes that occur immediately after Anna's disappearance and thereby link the water as a metaphor of unbounded desire to death. The sound of the sea-born wind is accentuated when a storm brews as Sandro and Claudia search for Anna after the initial sequence of music, and then again at night when, as they take refuge in a fisherman's hut, Claudia dons Anna's dress; the wind continues to blow when the couple couple meets in the early morning on the cliff top in the rain.

But if these sounds of nature are linked to the figuration of a contingently feminine, incipiently deadly desire, so too are the mechanical sounds of engines. The noise of the open-top sports-car carrying the two women into town that delivers Anna to her lover at the film's opening and then takes the women to the boat trip as their hair blows in the wind, evoking the irrepressible urgency of desire. The relentless drone of the boat engine as the holiday-makers approach the island seems to add a further element of slow-burning suspense to the claustrophobic scenes of sexual tension on the boat. It is the off-screen throb of the fisherman's boat that offers a vague promise that Anna might be still alive. Later in the film, the sound of the train crossing the countryside in long shot but then suddenly rushing, loudly and threateningly, very close by, as Claudia and Sandro make love in the open air, connects their lovemaking to the broader pattern of desire. All these sounds are characteristically, if amorphously, linked to the sense of sexual tension and the wandering or migratory desire that characterizes it, and which is centrally connected to female sexuality.

In his conception of the sound design of *The Birds*, Hitchcock, I would suggest, paid close attention to Antonioni's innovative use of sound in *L'Avventura*. As Elizabeth Weis first pointed out, Hitchcock creates a complex network of relationships between the sound of nature (the birds), machine sounds (the sound of the sports car, the boat engine, and the electronically produced bird squawks), and human sounds.[31] Antonioni's use of the sports car and boat engine to signal the insistent and provocative desire of the wandering woman seems directly transplanted to the figuration of Melanie as she swoops down like a bird to Bodega Bay in her open-topped sports car, and then makes her way by boat, again skimming over the water like a bird, accompanied by the loud putt, putt, putt of a big, black, outboard motor. Hitchcock's complex deployment of the "bird" analogy and the way in which he bestowed avian quality upon Tippi Hedren both in the publicity for the film and in the film itself link the contagious and migratory desire to nature. The fact that this desire is expressed through man-made sounds forges a connection between Melanie's own impulsive desire and the relentless assault of the birds, because the sounds of the birds are also evoked through man-made sounds. Our sense of the gigantic massing and hence monstrosity of the birds is created through an insistent, all pervasive, pulsating electronic "sound curtain" in such a way that the desire that is expressively attached to the figure of the wandering woman through the mechanical sounds that accompany her flight over land and water are linked, via Hitchcock's employment of electronic sounds, to the figuration of the birds in their assault.

Anxieties of Influence

The story of *The Birds* and the backstory of the making of the film converge in ways that have been speculated upon extensively.[32] In "falling in love" with Tippi Hedren/Melanie Daniels, if this is indeed what happened, Hitchcock himself had succumbed to the contagion of a mimetic desire that he brought into being. What greater split between subject and object could there be than Tippi Hedren and Melanie Daniels, the wandering woman that Hitchcock imagined Tippi to be. He created in Hedren/Daniels a character, vain and capricious, who was defined by an external appearance and mode of comportment he fussed over daily in his role as director and beyond, and what could Hedren do other than to play to the best the role that she was contracted to perform. The more Hedren learned from Hitchcock and succumbed to his every direction, the more she became the object of his veneration, and he the object of her disdain. But this only fuelled Hitchcock's martyrdom at the altar of "love." During the shooting of *Marnie* on Valentine's day, Hitchcock, according to Spoto, sent his star a "long, bizarre, and impassioned telegram." He spoke of the legends of two martyrs named Valentine that he identified as himself; he wondered why as a martyr he should be singled out by the *Encyclopedia Britannica* to symbolize the festival of lovers; and "He concluded by reminding her of his martyrdom, which, he added, caused exquisite pain for the martyr 'Alfredus.' "[33] Hedren's emphatically real indifference could masquerade in Hitchcock's imagination for the indifference of coquettish desire, of a vanity provoked by his desire.

The artistic consequences of this contagion are visible in Hedren's superbly refined performances in *The Birds* and perhaps even more so in *Marnie* of a brittle, narcissistic femininity, with a hard shell but incredibly vulnerable inside. Its personal consequences were that Hedren was subject to the indignity of what would today be defined as sexual harassment in the workplace, and Hitchcock's fate was the same as that which, according to Girard, befalls all men who succumb to this mode of desire's contagion, for this form of desire only ever works when kept at a distance and is only ever skin deep:

> As the mediator approaches the desiring subject, coquetry disappears. The loved woman does not succumb to her lover's contagion. She devotes herself

to a secret disdain which is too intense for the lover's desire to be able to counterbalance. Thus desire, instead of raising the woman in her own eyes, lessens the lover in her opinion. The lover is relegated to the realm of the banal, the insipid, and the sordid where dwell objects who let themselves be possessed.[34]

We might also speculate that Hitchcock's imagination of Tippi Hedren as his lover was fuelled in part by the relationships that he observed on screen, for example, between Antonioni and his muse, as if such a relationship were somehow necessary to complete him as a film artist. It is surely a fact worth noting that in the film through which Hitchcock most desperately wanted to be acknowledged as an artist, a creative genius and an auteur, he allowed himself to be so profoundly influenced by another film that was deemed to be a great work of art in the eyes of the critics whose admiration he sought. It is also worth noting that this profound influence occurred through a work that seems so centrally about the nature of mimetic desire. It is but one further step to suggest that this contagion of influence spilled over into life, as Hitchcock not only imitated art but a certain idea of the European auteur that he envied: one whose love-life is entwined with his filmmaking practice.

Can a theory of influence based on mimetic desire be derived from this analysis? Of course, a theory of influence cannot be based on just one example, but fortunately such a theory already exists in the writings of Harold Bloom.[35] For Bloom, all creativity is based upon agonized, conflicted rivalry with the admired works that precede your own act of creation. According to Bloom, great art does not shirk from an engagement with the canon but emerges out of a creative misinterpretation of it Whether or not the details of Bloom's theory are correct—can one have "misinterpretation" without "interpretation," and so is *mis*reading actually the key?—the essential point Bloom shares with Girard is that creativity emerges out of imitation and rivalry. This idea is amply born out by Hitchcock's entire career in appropriating and adapting the work of others, and is fittingly manifest, most intensely, when the very question of Hitchcock's status as a creative artist is most at stake in the creation of *The Birds*.

Italian cinema, and Antonioni in particular, proved to be an extraordinary resource to Hitchcock at a pivotal moment in his career, allowing him to recharge his creative batteries and recapture some of the inspiration that he found in the German expressionism of his youth. Hitchcock's career had always balanced the influence of Weimar cinema and its concern with narrative ambiguity, "pure cinema," sexual transgression, and stylization, with the moral suspense, taut narrative construction, and the character-centered agency of Hollywood melodrama, whether the picaresque male adventure story or the female-centered domestic melodrama. In Antonioni's films he perceived an intensification of his own preoccupations in a way that, in the manner of art cinema narration, foregrounded narrative ambiguity and stylistic expressivity, as well as the alchemy between camera and female performer. In *The Birds*, he sought to bring Antonioni's art-house experimentation into Hollywood film by taking as his subject the sexual agency of his female protagonist who is "provoked" by the look of the camera, and ambiguously linking that agency to the threat of assault, abstractly rendered as the threat posed by nature and identified with the gaze of the camera.

The influence of Italian art cinema, and Antonioni in particular, is undoubtedly present in Hitchcock's films after *The Birds*. Hitchcock specifically mentioned that he wanted to shoot the opening scene of *Marnie* in the Italian way: "I feel like we ought to cheat like they do in the Italian films and have nobody around if we can. Because otherwise we don't draw enough attention to the girl."[36] And he could have found inspiration for this in any number of scenes in *L'Avventura*, such as the town that Sandro and Claudia visit that is empty of all people, or, more specifically, the deserted train station where Sandro says goodbye to Claudia. But *Marnie* bears the influence of *L'Avventura* in more precise ways. *L'Avventura* is in part the story of a loss or transference of identity in which the character of Anna, whose motivation is not clearly defined and whose sexuality is ambiguous, becomes absorbed into that of Claudia. Claudia, at a certain point, as we have seen, wears Anna's dress and even dyes here hair black to correspond to Anna. *Marnie* too is a film that centers upon the story of a wandering woman with a mercurial identity. In a pivotal scene in the film, she changes her identity by washing the black dye out of her hair and emerging as a blonde. Furthermore, the sexual frisson between women triangulated with a man in *L'Avventura* and *The Birds* is developed further in *Marnie* in the relationship between Lil Mainwaring (Diane Baker) and Marnie (Tippi Hedren). While Lil seems to have designs on her brother-in-law Mark Rutland (Sean Connery) and perceives Marnie as a rival, their rivalry also bestows on their relationship an allegiance, and their interaction is treated with a peculiar kind of intimacy. Finally, *Marnie* is a film about a coercive male protagonist who blindly seeks the realization of his desire irrespective of the wants of the woman he pursues, purporting to know her wants better than she does herself. Sandro, in *L'Avventura*, is less extreme in imposing his will than Mark, and he is a weaker, more conventional character, but he is a model for Mark in the way he insists in his pursuit of Claudia. Perhaps there is a parallel as well in the endings, where in *Marnie*, as in *L'Avventura*, there is a tentative gesture toward a restoration of hope and healing at the end of a story largely under the shadow of trauma.

Yet *Marnie* also illustrates a bedrock of affinity between Antonioni and Hitchcock that goes beyond influence. I have already noted the uncanny parallels between *L'Avventura* and *Psycho*. There are, equally, striking affinities between *Marnie* and *Il Deserto Rosso* (*Red Desert*, 1964) that Ian Cameron and Robin Wood have pointed out, even though direct influence is clearly not possible.[37] Both stories feature a deeply afflicted woman whom a man seeks to cure by forcibly imposing himself on her. In both, the woman's affliction affects her capacity to see. And in both films the "illness" of the central female character is arguably a form of resistance to the depredations of a patriarchal social order. The rapacious male characters in the films, both captains of industry, are symptomatic of the oppressive nature of this social order rather than an antidote to it. Both films, as McElhaney notes, offer only ambiguous cues for optimism that the protagonist might be cured of her illness.[38]

Color design is an area where affinity and influence is hard to measure. *Red Desert* and *Marnie* have stylistic commonalities in color design. They both use a strikingly elaborate non-naturalistic color scheme, where splashes of primary color stand out against gray or beige backgrounds. This color scheme is exemplified in the opening shot of both films: Monica Vitti's character walks with her son in the redemptive earth tones of green and brown against a desolate gray industrial wasteland, while Marnie in Hitchcock's film walks towards the vanishing point of a desolate gray station marked out from the environment only by the yellow purse she carries. Yet, while Hitchcock was clearly a sophisticated colorist in his own right, Antonioni's approach to color design is also arguably evident in Hitchcock's late films, for example *Torn Curtain* and *Frenzy*, in the manner that gray or beige landscapes, often framed through windows, denote an alienated, modern urban environment: East Germany and London, respectively.

Even as Hitchcock's encounter with Italian art cinema promised a renewal of his career, that renewal was short lived in spite of the moderate box office success of *Marnie*. At a time of increasing uncertainty in an industry faced with declining audiences, Hitchcock found himself constrained in the projects he could pursue. Particularly poignant in this respect is the unrealized project *Kaleidoscope* (also called *Frenzy*), which Hitchcock conceived as a sympathetic portrait of a serial killer, and which he sought to develop between 1964 and 1967, first with Robert Bloch, author of the novel *Psycho*, then with his erstwhile collaborator Benn Levy.[39] Directly inspired by the hand-held camera work, location shooting, and sexual explicitness of Antonioni's *Blow-Up*, he proposed to shoot the film entirely from the point of view of the killer himself, utilizing extensive hand-held camera work and location shooting on the streets of London. Some of the inspiration for this film arguably made its way into the film he made as *Frenzy* in 1972, where location shooting on the streets of London plays a significant role, but stylistically the completed *Frenzy* lacks the innovation of the unrealized project. A decade that seemed to promise innovation and experimentation under the influence of Italian art cinema ended with *Torn Curtain* and *Topaz* (1969), which in spite of bravura sequences of "pure cinema" repeated the well-trod ground of the cold-war spy thriller. His final work, *Family Plot* (1976), while in some respects a return to form, is also a return to earlier traditions of the comedy thriller that owes little to his encounter with art cinema. This is why it is tempting to see *The Birds*, which was originally planned to be shot after *Marnie*, less as a new beginning than as a culmination of his work. It is at once a return to origins that synthesizes art cinema and genre cinema in a manner that is comparable to the way in which he had earlier embraced expressionism, and a concluding work that constitutes, in its art cinema abstraction, the final summation of Hitchcock's way of thinking in cinema.

Notes

I am greatly indebted to my colleague and collaborator Sid Gottlieb for furnishing me with the two main examples from De Sica and Antonioni that inspired this paper, and for his feedback on earlier versions. Thanks also to John David Rhodes and David Forgacs for giving me the opportunity to develop an initial version at the Antonioni Centennial Conference at NYU (2012), and to Malcolm Turvey for reviewing the final draft.

1. See James Vest, *Hitchcock and France: The Forging of an Auteur* (New York: Praeger, 2003).

2. Patrick McGilligan, *Alfred Hitchcock: A Life in Darkness and Light* (New York: Harper Collins, 2003), 533.

3. Robert Kapsis, *Hitchcock: The Making of a Reputation* (Chicago: University of Chicago Press, 1992), 78.

4. See John Hellman, "*The Birds* and the Kennedy Era," *Hitchcock Annual* 17 (2011), 101-02.

5. Quoted in Patrick McGilligan, *Alfred Hitchcock*, 681.

6. See Donald Spoto,*The Dark Side of Genius* (New York: Da Capo Press, 1999), 484-85, and Steven DeRosa, "Writing with Hitchcock," online at htttp://www.stevenderosa.com/writingwithhitchcock/italian connection.html; and Sidney Gottlieb, "Unknown Hitchcock: The Unrealized Projects," in Richard Allen and Sam Ishii-Gonzáles, eds., *Hitchcock: Past and Future* (New York: Routledge, 2004), 85-106.

7. John Orr, *Hitchcock and Twentieth-Century Cinema* (New York: Wallflower Press, 2005), 72-79.

8. See for example, Frank Tommasulo, "You're Tellin' Me You Didn't See: Hitchcock's *Rear Window* and Antonioni's *Blow Up*," in David Boyd and R. Barton Palmer, eds., *After Hitchcock: Influence, Imitation, and Intertextuality* (Austin: University of Texas Press, 2006), 145-72.

9. David Bordwell, *Narration in the Fiction Film* (Madison: University of Wisconsin Press, 1985), 205-27.

10. Mark Betz, *Beyond the Subtitle: Remapping European Art Cinema* (Minneapolis: University of Minnesota Press, 2009), 93-178.

11. For discussion of the process of script revision, see Evan Hunter, *Me and Hitch* (New York: Faber and Faber, 1997); Robert Kapsis, *Hitchcock: The Making of a Reputation* (Chicago: University of Chicago Press, 1992), 73-80; Bill Krohn, *Hitchcock at Work* (New York: Phaidon, 2003), 240-62; and Walter Raubicheck and Walter Srebnick, *Scripting Hitchcock*: Psycho, The Birds, *and* Marnie (Champaign: University of Illinois Press, 2011), 64-74.

12. For further comments on perverse agency in *Marnie*, see the essay by David Greven, "Intimate Violence: *Marnie* and Queer Resilience," in the present issue of the *Hitchcock Annual*, 107-48.

13. Joe McElhaney, *The Death of Classical Cinema: Hitchcock, Lang, Minnelli* (New York: State University of New York Press, 2006), 89.

14. Raymond Bellour, *The Analysis of Film* (Bloomington: Indiana University Press, 2001), 28-67.

15. Richard Allen, "The Sound of *The Birds*," forthcoming in *October* (Winter 2013). For further detailed analysis, see James Wierzbicki, "Shrieks, Flutters, Vocal Curtains: Electronic Sound/ Electronic Music in Hitchcock's *The Birds*," *Music and the Moving Image* 1, no. 2 (2008): 10-36.

16. See Michel Chion, *Film, A Sound Art*, translated by Claudia Gorbman (New York: Columbia University Press, 2009), 165-71.

17. See Hellmann, "*The Birds* and the Kennedy Era," 112-14.

18. Linda Williams, *Playing the Race Card: Melodramas of Black and White from Uncle Tom to O.J. Simpson* (Princeton: Princeton University Press, 2001).

19. André Bazin, "Hitchcock vs. Hitchcock," in Albert J. LaValley, ed., *Focus on Hitchcock* (Englewood Cliffs, NJ: Prentice Hall, 1972), 69.

20. François Truffaut, *Hitchcock*, revised ed. (New York: Simon and Schuster, 1984), 261-62.

21. René Girard, *Desire, Deceit and the Novel: Self and Other in Literary Structure*, translated by Yvonne Freccero (Baltimore: Johns Hopkins University Press, 1976), 99. In "To-night 'Golden Curls': Murder and Mimesis in Hitchcock's *The Lodger*," forthcoming in the journal *Contagion*, Sanford Schwartz argues that Hitchcock's third film, which is a source for so many others, provides a textbook anticipation of Girard's theory of mimetic desire.

22. Jean Paul Sartre, *Being and Nothingness*, trans. Hazel E. Barnes (London: Methuen, 1969), 364-412.

23. Girard, *Desire, Deceit and the Novel*, 105.

24. The *locus classicus* of this traditional understanding where woman is cast as the passive object of the male gaze is Laura Mulvey, "Visual Pleasure and Narrative Cinema," *Visual and Other Pleasures* (Bloomington: Indiana University Press, 1989), 14-26.

25. Stanley Cavell, *The World Viewed* (Cambridge: Harvard University Press, 1979), 24. The Wandering Woman could also be seen as another figuration of Cavell's "unknown woman." See Stanley Cavell, *Contesting Tears: The Hollywood Melodrama of the Unkown Woman* (Chicago: University of Chicago Press, 1996), and William Rothman, *The "I" of the Camera: Essays in Film Criticism, History and Aesthetics* (New York: Cambridge University Press, 1988),152-73.

26. Lee Edelman describes the importance of this scene for interpreting *The Birds* in "Hitchcock's Future," in Richard Allen and S. Ishii-Gonzalès, eds., *Hitchcock: Centenary Essays* (London: BFI, 1999), 244-45.

27. See, for example, Margaret Horowitz, "*The Birds*: A Mother's Love," in Marshall Deutelbaum and Leland Poague, eds., *A Hitchcock Reader* (Ames: Iowa State University Press, 1986), 279-87.

28. See Bill Krohn, *Hitchcock at Work*, 259.

29. William Rothman, *Hitchcock — The Murderous Gaze* (Cambridge: Harvard University Press, 1982).

30. See René Girard, *The Scapegoat*, translated by Yvonne Freccero (Baltimore: Johns Hopkins University Press, 1986).

31. Elizabeth Weis, *The Silent Scream: Alfred Hitchcock's Soundtrack* (Rutherford, NJ: Fairleigh Dickinson University Press, 1982), 136-47.

32. See Spoto, *The Dark Side of Genius*, 451-76, and *Spellbound by Beauty* (New York: Three Rivers Press, 2009), 243-77; and *The Girl* (2012), directed by Julian Jarrold.

33. Spoto, *The Dark Side of Genius*, 469-70.

34. Girard, *Desire, Deceit and the Novel*, 107.

35. See in particular, Harold Bloom, *The Anxiety of Influence: A Theory of Poetry*, 2nd ed. (New York: Oxford University Press, 1997).

36. Tony Lee Moral, *Hitchcock and the Making of Marnie* (Lanham, Maryland: Scarecrow Press, 1992), 125.

37. Ian Cameron and Robin Wood, *Antonioni* (London: Praeger, 1968), 120-21.

38. See Joe McElhaney, *The Death of Classical Cinema*, 118.

39. See Steven DeRosa, "Writing with Hitchcock," online at http://www.writingwithhitchcock.com/frenzy.html; and Gottlieb, "Unknown Hitchcock."

Contributors

Richard Allen is Professor and Chair of Cinema Studies at New York University. His most recent publications are *Hitchcock's Romantic Irony* (Columbia University Press, 2007), and (with Ira Bhaskar) *Islamicate Cultures of Bombay Cinema* (Tulika Press, 2009).

After some years teaching in S.t Louis and then Ireland, Charles Barr is now based again in England as Professorial Research Fellow at St. Mary's University College, Twickenham. His book on *Vertigo* in the BFI Classics series has recently been reissued in expanded form. *Hitchcock: Lost and Found*, co-authored with Alain Kerzoncuf, will be published in 2014.

John Bruns is Associate Professor of English and Director of Film Studies at the College of Charleston, where he is also a faculty affiliate of the Women's and Gender Studies Program. He received his Ph.D. from the University of Southern California and is the author of *Loopholes: Reading Comically* (Transaction Publishers, 2009). He is currently working on a project entitled *People, Places, and Things: Navigating the Hitchcock Landscape*. His work has appeared in *Film Criticism, Journal of Narrative Theory*, and *New Review of Film & Television Studies*.

David Greven is Associate Professor of English at the University of South Carolina. His books include *Psycho-Sexual: Male Desire in Hitchcock, De Palma, Scorsese, and Friedkin* (University of Texas Press, 2013), *The Fragility of Manhood: Hawthorne, Freud, and the Politics of Gender* (Ohio State University Press, 2012), *Representations of Femininity in American Genre Cinema: The Woman's Film, Film Noir, and Modern Horror* (Palgrave, 2011), *Manhood in Hollywood from Bush to Bush* (University of Texas Press, 2009), and *Men Beyond Desire: Manhood, Sex, and Violation in American Literature* (Palgrave, 2005). He is on the editorial board of *Cinema*

Journal, Genders, and *Poe Studies,* and is currently at work on a book about post-millennial Hollywood masculinity called *Ghost Faces.*

Amy Sargeant has written widely on British silent and sound cinema. Her publications include *British Cinema: A Critical History* (BFI, 2005), *The Servant* (BFI, 2011), and *British Historical Cinema: History, Heritage and the Costume Film* (Routledge, 2002), co-edited with Claire Monk. She currently teaches in the London Program of the Tisch School of the Arts, New York University.